TIPS ON AUDITIONING

IDEAS FOR ACTORS

Paige Klopfenstein

Tips on Auditioning

Ideas for Actors

Jon Jory

Smith and Kraus Publishers   2015

ISBN: 978-1-57525-895-9
Library of Congress Control Number: 2015947591

Typesetting and layout by Elizabeth E. Monteleone

Cover by Borderlands Press

A Smith and Kraus book
177 Lyme Road, Hanover, NH 03755
editorial 603.643.6431 To Order 1.877.668.8680
www.smithandkraus.com
Printed in the United States of America

*This work is dedicated to
Andrew Tsao, Victor Talmadge, VC Heidenreich,
Janet Zarish, Robyn Cohen, Jenny Mercein,
Gale Springer, Steve Woolf, Heidi Kettering,
and my dear friend Deb Monk,
who have been kind enough to tell their secrets.*

TABLE OF CONTENTS

STAGE, MUSICAL THEATRE, FILM, TELEVISION,
COMMERCIALS, TRAINING PROGRAMS
USER MANUAL

You could read the tips start to finish or simply browse until your interest is caught like lightning in a bottle. Not every tip will be useful to every reader, no matter what the author may think. What I imagine is that different tips may apply given whatever material you have chosen and where your actor-head is at the moment. You could think of it as a book of spells responsive to your current needs. The book covers auditions for the stage, musical theatre, film, television, commercials, and to get into school training programs. It hopes to be very, very practical.

Because audition is also simply acting, there is a reminder section on applicable acting basics.

Finally there are seventy-five new audition pieces and each is accompanied by a director's note to assist in its performance.

In a long career I have probably seen a quarter million auditions and this little book devolves from that fascinating experience.

—Jon Jory

THEY

What Do "They" Look For? (I)

- Are you confident? Does your manner <u>make us believe</u> <u>you have a right to be there</u>? This is a "stage presence" issue. *I am worthy*

- Do you understand and have a point of view toward the material you have chosen? In other words, what is the piece about? Why is it dramatic or funny? If your performance misjudges the piece we take it to be a failure of intelligence or taste.

- Do you actually have a real thought process as you perform the piece or are you just "saying" it. A good thought process while you act is a big audition plus.

- <u>Is it clear that your character wants something</u>? Is what your character wants a good choice for the piece? The more this is <u>true moment to moment</u> the more impressed we are.

- Are you, within the context of the piece believable? When your work is not recognizable as believable, when the emotions are faked, it scares the "bejabbers" out of us. Without a bottom line belief in what you say we don't want you in our play.

What Do "They" Look For? (II)

- Do you have a mind/body connection? Does what you think create gesture and movement that seems apt? What does your physicality add to the piece?

- Is your voice one we would want to listen to over the course of two hours? Do your vocal problems (and articulation) seem fixable in the short term?

- Is there rhythmic and vocal variety? This means an honest use of loud and soft and fast and slow, to put it bluntly. Is there any sense that this actor is a jazz musician with words?

- Do you have your own version of charm? Charm being defined as that which makes the actor in front of you likable. Yes, there are many versions but the quality itself is crucial. A charm-killer is working too hard with unjustified, non-absorbable energy.

- Did you pick material that shows off your particular talent? Not understanding certain material isn't good for you means a worrisome lack of self-knowledge.

WHAT DO "THEY" LOOK FOR? (III)

- Are you in shape? Do you care about your body and look? Are you, in a sense, proud of yourself? Your look is important to your castability.

- Is your vocabulary of gesture limited or expansive? Is your gestural work simply practiced or does it seem spontaneous. Is there anything surprising about it?

- Do you seem like a good and giving person? Yes, really! I'll be in the rehearsal room with you for a month or more. Does it seem like I'll enjoy the work with you?

- Do you seem to have impulses or does it seem you're doing it for the hundredth time exactly the same way? Are you creatively present?

- Does the work you are doing seem creative or surprising in some way? I'll even buy eccentric. What is there in your audition that would make me pick you rather than somebody else?

WHAT ARE THE PEOPLE AUDITIONING YOU THINKING? (I)

- "This chair is uncomfortable. My back hurts and I wish I had a sandwich." Yes, like most people we're thinking as much about ourselves as we think about you.

- "Why would he have that many piercings if he wants to be an actor?" Yes, we do ponder how you look and whether we like your look. It's not very evolved but it's a fact.

- "Why would she sit down the whole time?" Yes, we like people with a creative, grounded physicality. Acting is partly a physical sport. If you don't take care of your body, what else don't you take care of?

- "Very limited vocally." We have to listen to you for two hours in a play.

- "Seems personally hostile and remote." Hey, we have to be in the room with you for weeks of rehearsal.

- "What if I can't cast the part?" Yes, underneath our cool relaxed attitude we're a little desperate. We would be thrilled if you were good.

WHAT ARE THE PEOPLE AUDITIONING YOU THINKING? (II)

- "Looks too much like the woman in the other part." Yes, many times it's not just about quality. Unfortunately there are many factors you can't control.

- "She's good but is there enough acting energy for a part this big?" Yes, it's honesty plus energy. What you do needs to read to the back of the house?

- "She's skilled but is she believable?" Yes, believability is the actor's touchstone, however it is achieved.

- "But does she have comic sense?" the hardest thing to learn if it's not God-given. It just may not be your thing.

- "I like her, but we better check her references and make sure those references are good!" Try not to leave black marks behind you anywhere.

- "His work is so forced. For God's sake calm down!" Overuse of high energy makes the acting look amateurish. High energy is a garnish not an entrée.

What Are the People Auditioning You Thinking? (III)

- "I love him!" Yes, but you can't always tell that. On the other hand when they seem to like you it may just be good manners. Don't drive yourself crazy trying to suss out how you were received. You'll hear.

- "She has a great resume but . . ." They scan your resume to see if you've played good roles, to see if they know anyone who's worked with you and to make judgments about your level of experience. They put significantly more weight, however, on the quality of your audition.

- "He's wonderful but has limited experience." Sometimes they'll take the chance sometimes they won't. You'll have more experience next year. You can't have everything right away. *you arrive when you arrive*

- "She's just right, but what about the other woman we saw earlier?" Yes, you were better than 29 of the 30 other women they saw but there was that girl they saw earlier! That's why auditioning is a bitch.

- "He's not right for this role but he's perfect for the Tennessee Williams we're doing in March." Yes, sometimes you're auditioning for this play and then end up in the next one. That's why you audition every chance you get.

THE THEATRE'S CASTING AGENT

Most of the larger regional companies have someone on staff who organizes and has significant input into the theater's casting policies and calls. This person is separate from the New York or Los Angeles casting agent. If the theater is in Kansas City, she is a resident there, and while she will have other duties as well, casting is usually her most significant task. The theater's casting agent has the ear and respect of the artistic director and has probably been responsible for finding the casting agents the theater uses in New York and Los Angeles. Let's call her Rachel. Rachel arranges the coastal audition calls, chooses the audition studio, makes suggestions to the other casting personnel, brings in actors of her choice, and handles screening auditions when the artistic director absents himself. Get to know these people, stay in touch with them, and pay attention to them. All the power doesn't reside in New York.

DOES IT MATTER WHAT TIME YOU AUDITION?

I think so, but it's a little hard to quantify. Let me try doing it this way.

10:00 :

The upside is I'm fresh, energetic and more likely to give you feedback than in the afternoon. The downside is that I don't remember much about your audition by six p.m.

12:30 :

The bloom is off the rose. Unless you are awfully good or awfully bad I'm thinking more about lunch than about you. Hunger, unsurprisingly, tends to trump aesthetics.

1:00 :

> Back from a half-hour lunch and eager to cast the play. I have a better sense of what a good audition is comparatively than when I started but I have hope. In my view this is the best time to audition. I'm not wishing I had become a lawyer yet.

5:00 :

> Quitting time is six. I'm tired and the tiniest bit cranky. Unless you are among the best I've seen I basically stop thinking about you after thirty seconds (or earlier). You may be better than I think because my judgment is impaired.

WHAT I PERSONALLY LOOK FOR

- Have you come to play? Are you really willing to pretend or are you simply talking intelligently?

- Does your mind organically move your body?

- Do you understand what the text demands of you? More simply put, do you understand the text?

- How much talent do I sense here? Does it seem deep or shallow?

- Do I like your voice?

- Do you work too hard? Is the use of energy suitable? Is there enough energy to hold my attention?

- Would I like working with you or would you set my teeth on edge?

- What's creative about the work?

- Do you have some variety of charm?

- Are you forgiving about my eating my sandwich?

24

Jon Jory

What the Director Sees and Hears

- They clearly get how well you know the script.

- They get if you have charm.

- They measure you against their idea of the role.

- They think they can tell how smart you are.

- They think they can tell if you are well prepared.

- They know if they like your look.

- They are struck by your teaching them something about the role.

- They think they can tell if you're nice.

- They want to see if you can take direction.

- They measure you against people they know are already cast.

- They know if they like your voice.

- They think they can tell if you know what you're doing. Do you have the "chops?"

- They want your brain connected to your body.

- They see you handle the social situation of auditioning.

- They get your energy.

MATERIAL

BOREDOM

Shhh, don't tell my colleagues, they will deny what I'm about to say to the death. People watching auditions are bored, sometimes desperately bored.

Why?

You overwhelmingly see middling work. It's okay but not hirable or castable. You know this in the first twenty seconds and then have up to ten minutes to watch work you already know you can't use. It's mind numbing, and you have to pretend that you're interested. Of course this works wonders for the good audition.

What's the percentage of good auditions that I see? And by "good" I mean at least faintly usable for the role under consideration? I'd say, completely unscientifically, one in six. I also see some "good" auditions from actors wrong for the role but well worthy of future attention. Of the five out of six I know almost immediately I can't use, they are simply underprepared and I have no idea why they bothered to come. That's really boring. Sometimes they are very experienced actors who feel they are good enough to come in underprepared. Wrong!

Always come in prepared

The major mistake made by good actors doing bad to middling work is they don't understand what the necessities of the role are to make the play work. They don't understand what's needed situationally. "What exactly is this scene about?" is the question left unanswered.

The good news is, if you have prepared and know what the scene is about and perform it fully (and look a little bit like what's wanted) it's easier than you think to go down to the wire as a finalist. Boredom banished.

CHOOSING MATERIAL

The basic rules are:
1. No audition piece (no way, never, nuh-uh) should run more than one minute thirty seconds. Actually,

a minute fifteen is better. By then they have seen your strengths and are spending time itemizing your weaknesses. Leave them wanting to see more.

2. Use pieces that are in or near your own age range. You don't have the life experience to play fifty-year-olds. Really.

3. Try not to use pieces you know or suspect are wildly overdone. Your Shakespeare should not be Puck, Viola's ring speech or Launce's tale of his dog.

4. Self-written pieces are fine if you write well.

5. Contrast in two pieces is an obvious plus. It answers the "what else can she do?" question.

6. Don't do what you can't do. If your comedy sense sucks don't do comedy.

7. No. No, no, no. Don't do a new piece that isn't well prepared just to do a new piece.

8. And, please God, don't do a highly emotional piece if you have to fake all the emotion.

9. Find pieces that show off your strengths. If you don't know your strengths, ask someone you can trust.

10. Where do I find pieces? There are dozens, if not hundreds of books containing audition pieces. There are seventy-five contemporary audition pieces near your age range in the book you are holding. For Shakespeare get "*Soliloquy: The Shakespeare Monologues*" published by Applause Books. There's one for men and one for women.

HOW MANY AUDITION PIECES SHOULD I HAVE PREPARED?

Six:

    Shakespeare dramatic
    1 Shakespeare comic or romantic
    1 contemporary dramatic
    1 contemporary comic

1 contemporary romantic
1 contemporary complex language

You need this repertoire kept up and in good shape for five or six years after you leave school. Often when I like your work very much I ask for one more piece to make sure of my opinion. Sometimes, even with very mature actors, when I am auditioning small roles who really don't have a two-minute scene in the play, I'll ask to see an audition piece so I can judge quality of their acting. Many actors lose that job because they haven't needed to have an audition piece for many months or years and can't remember the ones they used to do. Keep at least one Shakespeare and one contemporary piece in working order even if you're now using a walker. My advice would be to set aside a half hour a month to polish up those party pieces. If you are in your early to mid-twenties you will need all six of those pieces on a fairly regular basis. Don't lose a crucial job for lack of them.

WHAT'S YOUR AUDITION SCENE OR PIECE ABOUT?

So much of the impact of your audition depends on how you realize your part in the story being told. Here are questions you need to answer before you proceed to the acting.

- You are talking to whom why?

- What is the outcome you want to occur from talking to this person?

- What is the nature of the relationship you have with this person?

- Why is this moment important to your character? Are you making it sufficiently important?

- Are you making the mistake of playing the "emotion" rather than the want?

- What tactics are you using to get what you want?

  A) Is there (as there should be) more than one?

- What are the most important moments?

  A) How will you make them important?

- Are you devoting sufficient concentration and energy to your pursuit of what you want?

- Where are the moments of subtext (where what you say has a different meaning underneath the words) and are you playing that subtext?

- Do you get what you want? Do you fail to get what you want? What is your character's reaction to winning or losing?

HOW LONG, OH LORD, HOW LONG?

Short. Solo audition pieces need to be short. Absolutely no longer than ninety seconds apiece. Really, no more. No kidding. No more! The reason is simple, if you're good we know that in the first minute, and why take the chance of wearing out your welcome? If you're not so good on that particular day we have a lot of of time to solidify our opinion. Ninety seconds is fine. Cut the piece to that length, and that includes Shakespeare. If you have an excellent sixty second piece, so much the better. If we really want to see more we'll ask you for another piece. Make sure you have one. I have very, very seldom changed my opinion for the better after ninety seconds. The talents I would like to see at a longer length are less than 2 to 3% of the auditions that pass before me. Enough said.

Jon Jory

THE SHAKESPEARE PIECE

Okay, I give up, you can't teach Shakespeare performance in a hundred and fifty words. However, I will offer some advice to the novice who has to audition for the Wilderness Shakespeare Festival and Pastry Shop on Wednesday.

1. Force yourself to translate the piece into your own English (not Shakespeare's) on a sentence by sentence basis. It would be a truism that if you really don't know what you're saying the acting will suck. Then do the piece several times in your English before you go back to Shakespeare's. It works.

2. Keep sentences together. Strange pauses in the midst of Shakespeare poetry (or prose) make the work almost impossible to follow.

3. Just as you must learn the lines to perform, decide exactly where you can breathe (the breathe score) without breaking up Shakespeare's mighty lines and images.

Do these three things plus strongly playing what the character wants in the moment will allow you to acquit yourself well. Oops, have to go, the Shakespeare scholars are coming up the hill carrying torches and clubs.

BREAKING DOWN AUDITION WORK

- If the piece is from a play, read the play twice *without* making acting decisions. Just let the story sit in you.

- Now write down three things that interest you about the character you are playing.

- List at least ten given circumstances. (Re-read the basics section in this book). Which of these givens need to be present and visible in your presentation of the piece?

- Re-read your piece to identify its central overall point. What is the key sentence or sentences? How will you make those pop out?

- What is the emotion in the piece that you might over-use and fake? Warning: it's best to underplay emotional content in auditions, as you don't have the whole play carrying you.

- Act the piece with an emphasis on its characters' logic.

- Visualize the physical structure of your audition. Call it the blocking if you will. Now cut that in half and practice it. Warning: do not wander back and forth!

- Make sure you are not playing in the same rhythm and tone!

- Now do the piece twice a day for a week.

- Go back over the proceeding nine points.

- Rehearse it once a day until it's time for your audition.

Look Out For the Audition Piece That Is Simply a Story

The "good story" is very seductive to actors looking for audition material. Yes, the story about your mom ending up dating the police officer who arrested her for drunken driving is great entertainment over a beer but is it truly dramatic? What makes that story good theatre or film or television is the "why" behind why it is being told now (in the script). It's dramatic if it is being told at her wake after she's been killed driving drunk. The point of the story might be that her drinking should have been stopped by the family much earlier. The "funny" story then has a very bittersweet bite. So, if your audition piece is a story out of the characters past, you play the action which is what the character hopes to gain by telling the story. Self-contained stories are made riveting by the reasons for telling it. Play that and give the story more flavor and relevance.

AGE APPROPRIATE

Ah, the pain of seeing eighteen-year-olds do Falstaff and thirty-five year old actresses do Juliet! Really, it's excruciating. You are way, way out of your league. Worse, it's a testament to making bad choices and lacking a clear sense of yourself, and who wants to cast a human with those problems? In an audition for a masters program in which I was teaching, a young actor not only did Lear's death scene (very, very badly) but appeared in a costume of his own devising. Yes, it was touching and my heart went out to him but . . . I won't even go into it!

Remember the point of an audition: you are being hired for what you can do, not for a fantasy regarding what you can do. If you are auditioning for, let's say, a Shakespeare Festival producing *Much Ado About Nothing* and *Taming of the Shrew* in rep and you are twenty-two years old, you are not likely to be cast as Beatrice or Kate. Why? Beatrice has been around the block in a way no twenty-two year old is likely to. She definitely in Elizabethan terms, should have been married years ago. As to Kate, it frankly demands acting skills and power twenty year olds don't have. Why audition for roles you're not going to get? You should be auditioning for Hero in *Much Ado* and Bianca in *Taming of the Shrew*. Should I be having to say this? Apparently, yes. Auditions are not the arena for wish fulfillment.

CONTRASTING PIECES

Hmmm. I'm almost tempted to say this is an old wives tale, much like the idea that garlic must be harvested at full moon if it's going to protect you from vampires. The idea of "contrasting" has come to mean one comic and one dramatic audition piece. Now people with second-rate comic skills are going to suffer in that format. Most actors are not equally good at both.

Secondly, really funny speeches are scarce as hens' teeth, plus very few stage comedies are written any more. Those kinds of writers now work in television. Why would you do a third rate comic speech? I suggest that yes, the pieces should differ but one could be a woman talking to her injured child in a hospital and the other could be a romantic piece from Jane Austin's *Pride and Prejudice*. You want to show two different sides of your talent but (unless you are auditioning for a Shakespeare Festival) one doesn't have to be the Bard. You're trying to show you can handle complex language and no one will arrest you for doing Moliere, or Austen, or Sophocles instead of Shakespeare. Do two pieces where the characters have strongly different objectives in very different circumstances.

Most importantly do two pieces you will be very, very good at. A theatre or training program that will turn you away after you do first rate work simply because one wasn't comic, or you did a contemporary verse speech rather than Shakespeare, is the home of pedants or fools. Good work is what's wanted. Do that.

The Good Audition Piece

There's the search for the Holy Grail, the search for the Fountain of Youth, and the search for the great audition piece. What are its qualities?

- You love it. It makes you laugh, it touches you, it speaks for you. You adore the writing. If the piece itself doesn't attract you, forget it.

- You know what you do well. Is this a vehicle for you?

- The situation in the piece is crystal clear within twenty seconds.

- It has a strong present action. The character *needs* something. If it's a good story, there's a point beyond the narrative.

- It allows for both movement and stillness.

- It embodies some sort of passion.

- It's a part you could play now, not fifteen years from now.

- It isn't currently being overexposed. Nine other people won't do it the same day.

- It's a piece that demands stage energy, mental, physical, or both.

- You feel attractive doing it.

THE ROOM

ENTERING THE ROOM

Remember, you are for the duration in the director's home and you are the guest. You don't have to bring a "hostess" gift, but other than that all the usual courtesies apply. You dress nicely, or at least neatly. Don't strew your stuff all over the floor. Put your backpack by the door where you will remember to take it with you when you leave.

It's a kindness to mention your name as in "Hi, I'm Carla" because your auditioners are desperately trying to locate you on their list. Keep in mind that most people don't shake hands anymore, but if a hand is offered steel yourself and shake it.

If, perchance you know one of the people auditioning, you don't rush across the room and embrace them uttering cries of delight. It's embarrassing for everyone else. Give them a wave and a smile and get on with it. The people auditioning you are on a tight schedule and are probably running late.

If you need to, move a chair as you announce your pieces or ready yourself to read from the script. Do not say you have a cold or have been in a skiing accident. Finally take two breaths to settle yourself and show your work.

LEAVING THE AUDITION

Do's
- Do say thank you.

- Take all your stuff. Forgetting something and having to come back isn't cool.

- If you have been reading for a role and have been given 'sides,' ask: "would you like the sides back?"

- You may leave the chair where you placed it. The next auditioner will re-position it.

- Leave in a positive mood. We don't want to deal with your self-criticism.

Don't

- If your audition has been cut short, don't ask if you may do more.

- Don't give an unasked for opinion of your audition.

- Don't attempt to engage the room in further conversation. If they initiate conversion respond.

- Don't ask when you will hear the response. Either your agent (if you have one) may enquire or after a week or so you may call or email.

- Don't exit the building immediately. Wait outside for five minutes to see if anything further is wanted.

What If the Person Before You Is In There a Really Long Time and There Is Laughter and Applause?

- You are not the person before you, you are you. Do what you do.

- You have studied the script, made decisions, done the piece a bunch of times and you're good. You are going to show them there is more than one way to do what they are asking to have done.

- If you are cooked, you're cooked, right? That's very freeing. You have little to lose. Do what you do fully.

- Okay, she must have done it well but she probably doesn't look right. Your chances are good.

- You are going to be so good that even if you don't get this part they will ask for you next time.

- I laugh sometimes not because it's funny but to encourage the actor. I may keep them in the room longer because they were my sister's roommate, or my director's wife. There's no way to know what went on in there or why. You can only control what you do.

FIVE MINUTES BEFORE

You're next. The body and mind go dormant. Your hands sweat. The first line evades you. You are suddenly reminded you could *Hah!* have been a nursing major. How do you marshall your forces?

Concentrate on the larger picture. What's happening in the scene from which your piece was plucked? What does she want? What is the tactic she is using to get it? Concentrate on the "want." Make sure it's strong enough to be interesting. Don't sit there practicing how to say the lines! That only puts your creativity to sleep.

Remind yourself you're good at this. If you're afraid you're not good enough, you're an actor, pretend you are. Now breathe. Three deep breaths. Hold the fourth. Three shallow breaths. Repeat. Concentrating on your breath focuses your mind.

Just before you go in the audition room stand up and shake out your body for five seconds. Enough. You're ready. Go through the door. Say hello. Now pursue what the character wants. You're good.

THE FLOOR, THE PIANO, THE WALLS, THE DOOR

So, you're either auditioning in a theatre or a rehearsal room. You know those spaces like the palm of your hand. You're home. Now use them for heaven's sake. How many auditions have I seen, oh Lord, where the actor stands in empty space and talks and stands and talks?

Get down on the floor, kneel, lie on your back and stare at the stars, prop yourself up on one elbow. Make that floor your friend. Fall on it, jump on it, hit it with your fist. And you have walls, right? Lean on them, slide down them, write on them with imaginary chalk. There's a door? Knock on it, start to open it, change your mind and shut it. There's a piano? Play a few notes or a phrase during the piece or scene. Sit on it, sit on the floor and lean against it.

You are allowed to use the space. Do it. Other people won't. I'm not talking about frantic choreography, I'm talking about a couple of moments while you're working. Physical moments that express what you're feeling, things that punctuate the speech. An audition takes place somewhere. You're not in a time warp, add details related to the space you're in. The things there are your props. Those watching will enjoy the spontaneity. Be where you are and do things inside it. Within limits.

YOUR SENSES IN THE AUDITION ROOM

Unfortunately most audition rooms and spaces are a little bit like sensory deprivation tanks. Horrible fluorescent light, work light, no light, ugly furniture (down to one chair), rugs that should be donated to disease control centers, forbidding walls . . . ugh. If you're doing monologues you are, on top of everything else, deprived of reaction and a human to talk to. No wonder so many auditions seem as spare and undecorated as the surroundings. Let's just say it's unaesthetic. So you need to create a sensory filling environment in your head and heart. Need I say that most people don't. You need to come prepared with inner images that can draw your senses out of hiding.

First you need to image what the material demands you see in the very first moment. And I mean that inner image needs sufficient detail: you see a farmhouse weathered to grey wood. One window has been plywooded over, one of the three steps up to the porch has decayed. Behind it a healthy stand of birch. The day is cloudy and dull. You feel a slight chill (play it). The path you are walking on is gravel (play it). You stop. A mangy pit bull stands looking at you too your left (glance at it). Now talk.

Senses II

You want to turn what you see, hear, touch and smell into acting. You need to create these sense producers in your head but you also need to make stage business out of them—back to the farmhouse (previous tip).

Hunker down. Amidst the gravel is a pure white stone (it's imaginary of, course) and while you are talking run your thumb over its shiny surface then toss the imaginary stone away.

Get up, brush your pants off, now rub your hands together. (You're still talking. Plus remember this is a stage audition not a film audition) Now focus on the guy staring at you from the porch with a vulture on his shoulder and a meat cleaver in his hand. Maybe you back up a tad to create more distance between you.

The idea is to wake up your senses and smell the manure. If you have the images and smells (maybe a nearby factory blows its noon whistle) you can turn them into concrete details that enrich your audition performance in film auditions such sensory work is not to create "business" but to deepen the sense of reality necessary to film performance.

That Chair

There isn't much to work with in an audition. There's you, your voice, your body, your mind and maybe some simple object in your pocket or bag and then, there's that chair. It's usually a folding chair, right? Ah, the auditions it has seen! You may be in Chicago or Cheyenne but that chair is there with you.

I'm watching the auditions. Most of the actors sit in the chair the same way, get up from the chair in the same way . . . over and over and over.

I do an exercise called "chair acting." I say to the actor, sit in the chair nine different ways. I count them off. Then I ask for nine more. They show me, in perhaps two minutes, eighteen ways to sit in the chair. Then I ask for nine ways to get up from the chair. I have never seen an actor who couldn't do the exercise.

Why is it that in auditions every actor sits in the chair the same way and get up from it the same way? It's the only prop/object they have and it goes for nothing in revealing the speech. What a waste.

That chair.

GETTING TO THE FIRST LINE

You arrived. You're in the waiting area. Look around you. Nervous actors. You're a little nervous, they are very nervous. They know they're not fully prepared. You know you are. Nice feeling. This is a human situation not a gladiatorial combat. Talk a little to someone who looks nice. Ask them a couple of questions, doesn't really matter what. Try to create a normal, non-hyper atmosphere for yourself. If you like quiet, get some. If you're rehearsed sufficiently you don't need to go over the piece, it's there. Establish a normal breathing pattern. Don't sit there worrying and holding your breath. They call you. Stand up, take a deep breath, release it, go into the room. Now, recognize where you are (might not be a room, might be a stage). Actually *see* the people who are there. Play a game where you try to describe what they were wearing after you leave. Be there. Say hello. Name the pieces you are doing. This is your time, the room belongs to you. Move the chair if you need to. Another deep breath. Release it. Think the characters thought that leads you into the first line. Don't rush. Don't be frantic. Begin the piece. You know how to do it.

DOING THE WORK

THE BLOOD SPORT

Acting is not competitive, thank God, it is cooperative. All of us in the harness of the play, pulling together, to make the story live. The only winning is the story well told. There is, however, one unredeemably competitive aspect of acting, the audition. To really do it well you need the mindset of an Olympian.

Winning, unfortunately is everything. You have to have killer instinct. All things being equal you plain old need to outwork the competition. You have to burn the midnight oil. You need to work longer hours than the others. We all know the story of Kobe Bryant the great basketball star who stayed after every home game to shoot a thousand jump shots. He had the will. *He wanted it.*

You will find, I fear, that there are superior talents to yours. They have an indefinable something you do not. But, lucky for us, their native talent makes them lazy and ripe for the plucking. Great auditioners *want it*. Their success is an act of will. Spend the extra time it takes to really understand the scene.

Examine and re-examine your choices. Do it until you're bored and then do it again. Your percentage of booking the job will increase in clear proportion to the elbow grease applied. Do it again.

DID YOUR BODY COME TO THE AUDITION?

I am particularly attracted to *full body* actors. This means what you think creates impulses visible as physicality. I'm not just talking about walking around, I'm talking about a body that just *has to* express thought. It's seen in the tilt of a head, a hand desperate to express an idea, a leg that expresses your deepest need, a waist that bends and on and on. Stillness, a crucial need to allow the words full effect but…I carefully note the actor whose body impulsively follows the thought. Stillness without impulse makes me very, very suspicious of going into the rehearsal room with that actor. It's like a painter who only uses shades of blue. That can be striking, can be beautiful but over two hours it cannot communicate the shades of meaning. I am hiring five things: your perception, your creativity, your thought process, your body and your voice. An audition that only shows me three of those is unlikely to result in casting. And to be blunt, auditions are not an abstract art form. The purpose of the audition is to get you cast. Don't forget to bring your body.

WHAT MAKES AN AUDITION STAND OUT?

- The audition is actually felt. It isn't simply a piece of acting that is part of an endless continuum of acting from which the actor could cut another piece for you if demanded.

- The actor is thinking. The words are produced from thought. The thought is primary and the words are its result.

- The material has been seriously considered and decisions have been made that illuminate the material. The result is that the actor actually cares.

- The body is alive to impulse. The words are reflected in the body. The body is fully contributive to the sense.

- The variety of thought produces rhythm that assists the sense. It's fast and slow and loud and soft in the service of the sense.

- There is a strong, even unusual sense of concentration. I am drawn into that concentration.

- I want to know and see more. It peaks my interest. And I love your voice.

52

FIRST ROUND, LAST ROUND

There was a boxer named Willie Pep who fought in the forties and kept at it 'til the sixties. Nicknamed "The will o' the wisp" he won (get this) 229 fights and lost eleven. When he was fighting in his mid-forties his strategy was to fight like a whirlwind for the first twenty seconds of the round, stay in clinches for two minutes and then explode during the last twenty seconds.

Why? "The judges don't remember the middle." He was fond of saying. He also put great emphasis on the first round and last round.

Pretty good advice for the auditioning actor. When you start, those of us behind the table aren't fully concentrated on you. We're finishing up our notes on the previous actor and are looking over your resume. You need to demand our attention immediately, with the key word being "demand." "Demand" is the combination of what the character wants, the deep need to get it, and the internal energy with which the "want" is pursued.

I am suggesting here that you put extra rehearsal into the first four sentences and the last four sentences so they are burned into the auditor's consciousness. There is a wonderful side benefit which is the boost to your confidence that starting well provides and your overall sense of well-being when you walk out having nailed the ending.

AUDITION ATTITUDE

You're not getting the fucking job, but you do get to act for 2 minutes.

We're lucky to do this. Hard as an acting career may be, it's a boon to life and spirit. An audition is acting. Creative, fascinating, selective and challenging. All our experience, craft and intuition is crammed inside an intensely short period of work. It's acting distilled. The only real measure of success is one's own feeling about it. It's like an archer releasing a single arrow to the target. We must enjoy it on that basis. How it is responded to does not define us. It's only an instant of growth. And, it has its own absurdity which we can enjoy. It isn't about whether we can act, it's about the release of that single arrow. We mustn't assume it to mean more. Buddah would approve. Think about it as ten minutes of growth. Should the archer be depressed about an outcome of so limited a demonstration? Of course not. Today you get to work at something you love. Do it. Be glad. Move on. The archer's life is full of hits and misses. You cannot have such a life without both. Enjoy the event. Learn from it. Feel glad for your participation. There is no way an audition can be tragic. It's a fascinating form but a limited one. You'll do this a thousand times, don't look for too much meaning. Enjoy the moment.

FOCUS

All right, so we all know we don't play the audition directly to one of the people watching us, right? It's simple. If you play to me, making eye contact, it becomes incumbent on me to act with you. If I'm thinking about my acting then I'm definitely not thinking about your acting. If I'm not thinking about your acting then why are you auditioning? No eye contact with the watchers while you're doing the audition. Now, a lot of people fixate on one spot in the middle distance and play most of the audition to that single spot. Play to your left foot, then play to the ceiling, then you can play to the first focus point again. Why? Endless focus on one spot denies thought process, inhibits physical impulse and . . . well it just doesn't seem like a human behavior. You sit, checking where you sit before you do so. You look behind you to see if anyone's listening. You check your nails to see if you remembered to clip them. One of the ways physicality is created in an audition is by changes of focus, and we want that physicality.

EMOTION

Real, felt emotion puts the actor in the top echelon of what I see on any given day in the audition room. How often do I get to see such believable emotion? Rarely. Maybe once out of thirty auditions. On a banner day twice.

Why is it so rare? It's pretty hard to walk into a small room or empty theatre where you know you are being judged, pick up a speech or scene in the middle of a play and have your emotions show up. What I do see a lot of is false, forced emotion mimicking the sound the actor feels accompanies the emotion in question. It strikes a manifestly false note that is devastatingly apparent. It damages your audition.

What to do? You know the speech is emotional but emotionally you are as cold as a halibut on ice. First of all, concentrate on what the character wants. I want you to go back to Tennessee with me to see Dad who is dying. Really want that. Want it badly. Play the want, not the emotion. If the emotion actually shows up it's a beautiful bonus. If it doesn't, playing a strong intent still creates a good audition. Most people, in most situations try not to show emotion. Use that. Wipe away a nonexistent tear. Fine. Take a pause to collect yourself. Good. Look down for a moment. Cool. Just don't fake it in an obvious way. Please!

AUDITION FEAR

You know what I mean. Your hands are wet. Your body, fearing to do something wrong is unresponsive. You are worrying about forgetting the lines. You're thinking, "Why even do the audition, I won't get the part." Face it, you're a mess. For one thing, you probably haven't spent enough time rehearsing. That's well within your control, fix it. If, say, you have done the pieces full-out eight times, double that. While spontaneity is delicious and impulse is exciting, your fear of auditioning may mean you have to play without. I sit down here, I get up here, I throw the script against the wall here.

Having a more specific battle plan will make it easier to deal with your nerves. Make sure there is both quick and slow in your audition and know exactly where the quick and slow are. Nerves often destroy your variety. Be direct, play the action, you don't need the false emotion.

Use a prop some of the time. You may be afraid to show your work but you damn well know how to sharpen a pencil. Really sharpen that pencil as you do the piece and you will feel calmer and more centered. Know exactly how you will end the audition: I say "bugger off." I break the pencil in half. I stand a second looking at the broken pieces. I drop them in front of me. I stare out over the audience for three beats. I'm done. I say "Thank you." I gather up my stuff and go. You win. Your nerves lose.

Two Beats And You're Done

This is a useful way to finish any audition whether it's a monologue or scene. Act the last line. Let's say for the sake of argument it's, "And I never saw her again." So, act the line and then keep acting for two beats after the line in silence. Maybe it goes this way, "and I never saw her again." Looks down at his hands. Lets his hands fall to his sides. Now you're done.

Be yourself. Look at those auditioning you and say, "Thank you." Always act for two more beats after the dialogue is complete, then stop acting, take a one beat pause and say, "Thank you." It draws a clear cut line between your work as a character and your return to the room as the person auditioning. *Finish* the audition, then return to the room. Then say, "Thank you." You don't rush. You allow your work to have silent impact.

If there is no bridge between acting and not-acting it seems as though you were never fully "in" the piece to begin with.

GESTURE

Yes, we love stillness. Be still. On the other hand I'm watching how your mind moves your body. Great stage acting has arms. Arms, as well as eyes, are the mirrors of the soul. Emotion is seen in the arms as well as the eyes. An acting audition where the actors' thoughts never moves their arms flat out scares me. Do I want an actor with no arms in rehearsal? Nooooo! Now you may have no problem here, but many do. So, what to do if you're not Italian or Caribbean by nature?

If you're in an acting stage where you're feeling a little tight, a little self-conscious, you're going to have to bite the bullet and plan a few gestures. I promise I won't tell Stanislavski and you're in pretty good company because Sir Laurence Olivier did!! A way to keep it spontaneous is the three gesture exercise.

Pick any three. For instance. 1) Hit your chest twice, 2) Point at something or someone, 3) Scratch your knee. Now do the audition piece and, in any order, make sure those three gestures are in it. It's magic. To someone watching it seems completely natural. Now pick three different gestures and do it again. Be brave, pick at least one big, full arm gesture. Open up. Problem solved, you've got arms.

PUNCTUATING

No, this isn't a discussion of the barbarous misuse of the semi-colon. This is about the time honored technique of fitting in the physical when you *aren't* talking. Every veteran actor does this instinctually but younger folks often don't realize its value. Here's the way it works:

Audition Fragment:

"Okay, I don't want to hear about it. And hey, don't leave your shoes all over the place. And were you going to get me coffee, or was that a dream?"

You can punctuate internally by using a slight pause to insert physicality as in "Okay, (takes a slight pause and runs comb through hair) I don't want to hear about it." (Sits at the end of the sentence . . .another way to punctuate) "And were you going to get me coffee, (throws hands over head in irritation) or was that a dream?" (Falls on floor in mock collapse.)

You get it, I'm sure. By using physicality on the punctuation and where you take a pause you protect the sense of the line. Now too much of this work can look mechanical. On the other hand, used with discretion you look more professional. You should try it on a piece you are currently working on. Let's say in a ninety-second audition piece you might use this physical punctuation three or four times.

The Blocked Audition

Don't be afraid to carefully block your piece. It isn't a complicated process and it will improve your work. For the sake of simplicity we'll use a four move structure. Let's say you have placed a chair center. Remember, there are endless ways to do this, this is only an example. I'm going to start you downstage of the chair and a little to the left, kneeling. After two or three sentences you stand up. Two or three sentences after that you bend over, pick up an imaginary coin and either pocket it or put it in your bag. Toward the end of the piece you go to the chair and sit. On the last piece of punctuation you cross your legs. Do it with a piece you have ready. Here's another one. Start behind the chair, hands on the back leaning forward. A bit later, straighten up and turn in a tight circle while you talk. A bit later walk downstage center. Finally, go to the chair and put one foot up on it. Four basic moves, right? Now make one up yourself. Now your audition has a physical side and, thank you Jesus, there's no hopeless wandering.

58

SPACE

First of all, I am too often asked at workshops how far away should you be from those auditioning you? If you are in a theatre, which creates a natural separation between audience and stage, you want to work about four feet away from the stage's edge. If in a room you should probably set up about eight feet away from the auditioner's table. Most of your work will be in the center area at about this distance but you may work part of the time as close as four feet away from those watching and as far away as twelve feet if you place your chair (if you are using one) eight feet away and center you can also work six to eight feet to the chair's left or right. (This is a little boring isn't it?).

The next thing about space is to use it. If you are doing two pieces and one is quite still or mainly settled in a chair, the next needs to show something of your use of the stage. (No, we're not talking about tumbling here, though your ability to do a standing backflip could have its uses.) Your body is driven by thought and emotion—let's see some of those moments. You can also use an imaginary ground plan. You rise from the chair and go upstage six feet to the imaginary refrigerator, open its imaginary door, walk ten feet downstage and put the imaginary Pepsi on an imaginary table. Really. Use some stage.

PERFORMING NOTES

There is an important difference between performing a play and doing an audition and it isn't simply length. The play is a story told through relationships, character and incident. The point is to fully realize the story and as an actor all your efforts should be bent toward that end. The audition is a competition in which each actor's skills are demonstrated in a way that could be made suitable use of in the play being cast. As a director I'm seeing if the actor has the chops and assists in telling the story. What are the "chops" I'm looking for? A voice the audience can listen to for two hours with pleasure. Articulation that assures me the actor can be understood. A body that responds to the actor's thought and situation. A body that makes intelligent use of space. A body that informs this particular role as I see it. A mind that informs the text with variety and surprise. A mind that has something to teach me about the role. And then, an emotional clarity in the situation the text places them in.

This means I am looking for answers to the following questions as I watch the audition:

- Is this actor's voice articulation a help or hindrance to this role?

- Is this actor's body a good storytelling instrument?

- How smart is this actor about the role in terms of its circumstances and necessities?

- Would I like to be in this actor's presence for two hours?

- Does the mind, body and voice combined interest and charm me?

- What are this actor's emotional capabilities?

    Now audition.

VOCAL ENERGY

Many actors at the sunrise of their career seem to let the words tumble out like dead flounders washing up on the beach. The words, my friends, are for the audience, and for the words to interest them they need a certain energy and élan. Limp arrows don't hit the target. Thus the same energy a boxer uses to deliver the punch (ah, a festival of metaphors) needs to be behind your words. The words are the punch. This same energy can be behind the words at any volume. A whisper can strike like a snake. Words must command attention. Do yours? Lines delivered without the above-described push signal the audience (or in this case the auditors) that nothing important is taking place and they can plan their trip to the grocery store. I shouldn't have to exert myself to hear you. You should do the work. Words are the slaves of your objective. If you want something enough it gives your words thrust and pop. Remember, I'm not saying, God help me, that it all has to be loud. NO, and again no. The softer you go, the more you need to bite those consonants, both beginning the word and ending it. Enjoy those words. Eat em' like candy.

ENERGY

The high energy audition: it snaps, it crackles, it leaps tall buildings in a single bound. But does it get you the part? Occasionally. That energy convinces us that you can take stage and deliver the payload of the script. It's a very, very good thing . . . used in moderation. Unmoderated energy (and I see it quite often) is painful to watch, hear and experience. The best energy isn't really actor driven, it's character driven. It occurs when in the situation the character can no longer contain herself. It's usually a burst that occurs when the heart can hold no more. Spend a day noticing when high energy occurs around you. How long does it last (dancing excepted)? It occurs, it explodes, it declines into normality. Do that. Yes, we want an actor who can dominate the stage and push the story out into the audience. We don't want a constant energy that pushes the audience out of the theatre. Find the moment in the piece where your energy cannot be contained, use it full force, then let it die back into your more complicated interpretation. Show the energy, don't blow the energy out. Just as there is no fast without slow, there is no energy without calm. Give us the mix.

The Most Important Moment

The most important moment in your audition, the one that defines what the piece is about, has to pop out of your work like a chorus boy out of a cake. You want to sear that moment into the memory of those who watch. If the audition is about your relationship to your father there is one sentence that best defines it. Let's say it's the line, "and then he walked out for the fifteenth and last time." Now how do we give that line the place of honor? How do we pop it out of all the talk?

• It's the moment where the emotion surges, and afterward is contained.

• There's a pause before it and pause after it.

• The piece has been mainly still and this line drives you out of the chair.

• It's a quick moment after some slower, more contained work.

• It's a slow, quiet moment after quicker, more energized work.

• It's the moment when you make direct eye contact.

You get the drift, I'm sure. The most important moment that contains the beating heart of your audition is . . . well . . . different than all the others. First find the piece-defining moment and then make sure your heart, your mind, your body and voice give it the special treatment it deserves.

Belief

The key. The base line. The necessity. We are looking for your simple belief in the character and situation you perform for us. Backflips, wild behavior, shouting and dancing are dandy if I (your auditor) feel they could happen in the circumstances, could happen with your Hamlet in this moment. Don't forget to remember what you know about life. Bring your street smarts with you. What might this character, in this moment *do* to get what she wants? We're not hoping you will solve the dilemma of belief by making all the acting tiny and quiet. We're hoping you want what the character wants so strongly that the need expresses itself in that backflip you've been longing to do. Let need drive behavior and belief results. Without basic belief inside situation almost no other acting skill satisfies. Build belief detail by detail. Where is she? What is she wearing? What does the person you're talking to look like? What happened just before your speech? What is your agenda? What would have to happen to make it the perfect outcome for you? What's the obstacle to getting what you want? What's the best tactic to get past the obstacle? Is it hot, cold, raining, blowing? Are you optimistic or pessimistic in the circumstances? How could you blow it? Questions build belief.

Oops

Ah, the dreaded moment when you have finally scored an audition with the Orlando Shakespeare Festival and after killing with your Iago you launch into Benedick and suddenly you have no idea what the next line is. None. Nada. Nil. What now, brave heart?

Well, actually there are some unwritten laws at play here. If you've only gotten two or three sentences in when you dry you can stop, smile charmingly and ask if you might start over? Please don't do that if you've already been toiling away for a minute or even thirty seconds. Why? Those watching you are on a tight schedule and, hey, it's also a little embarrassing. The further objection is when most people begin again they do it exactly the same way. Exactly. This unfortunately reveals you're not in the midst of a creative act but simply one of repetition. Not a tremendous credit to the actor's imagination and so much for being in the moment. So, you're a minute in and you are blank. Go back a sentence and see if that unlocks you. Breathe in and breathe out which may free your fried brain. Nothing? Simply say "Thank you" and consider the audition complete. If that was your first piece go on to the second. If it was your second go out and drown your troubles in a ginger-lemonade. Don't feel to badly, it happens to everyone and you handled it well. Probably it will never happen again. Some days the bear eats you.

THINKING

We're actually there to see you think. Thinking, you see, is the sexiest and most important thing an actor does in an audition. Language is the product of thought. Where's the thought? I watch transitions in an audition. How did the actor get from A to B? Where the actor doesn't even realize there is a B to get to, it's like watching a race driver miss the curve and hit the wall. Sometimes when the actor becomes a thoughtless zombie it's because they are going so fast their mind can't keep up with them. Sometimes it's because they are not really present, they are actually a recording. Sometimes it's because they are in the grip of ice-cold fear. Whatever the reason, it drives me out of casting them. The actor who is not present has a much harder time engaging us. We can admire them but we keep our distance and go home strangely unsatisfied. Whenever there is a change of subject, the mind needs to get from the coffee you spilled on your lap to your wish that the other person would not go home. It can take five seconds or a split second but the change of thought must exist. Mark in your script where it seems obvious you need to get from A to B, then think your way there when you perform. If you need to pause to think, pause. If you need to move to think, move. If you need to gesture to think, gesture. Look at it this way, no thinking no casting.

THE PAUSE UNDER FIRE

Yes, the pressures on. It's there inside you and, in addition, you're on the clock. The psychology of the actor is sometimes damaged by both pressures. "Maybe I'm not good enough" mixes with "I better hurry and get a lot done in a short time . . . faster, faster!" It's not a good recipe. One of the first losses that occurs in this mix is thought process, and when that happens its "robots on parade." The good audition maintains its humanity and that humanity gets lost in the speed. Slow down a little. Take the edge off and the acting gets richer. There's always a good pause available in the time you have. Take it and fill it with thought. Look for the moments where your character knows what will be said next will change the nature of the scene. Look for the pause where the character isn't sure how to phrase what she's going to say next. Look for the pause before your character changes the subtext. The actor needs to have a bullfighter mentality. Control your material don't let it control you. A little silence draws us in, makes us sit forward, and makes us anticipate your next move. Make sure your audition doesn't seem like a fire drill. You're interesting; take the time to show it.

TOO MANY DAMN PAUSES

Silence is golden, yes. It has a slew of useful aids to acting. Pause. I'm deciding. Pause. How can I put this? Pause. Once I say this I can't go back. Pause. You're going to hate this. Pause. I don't know what to say. Pause. And here's the big surprise. Pause. I want you to really get this. Pause. I'm going to hurt you. Pause. I'm going to kiss you. Etcetera. We want a little silence that speaks volumes in our audition. We just don't want a reflexive silence at every piece of punctuation. Many actors take a one or two beat pause at every period and a couple of interior pauses in every sentence. The pause is the garnish not he entrée. In most speeches you want to play units of thought not just sentences. A lot of actors don't realize they are taking a dozen pauses in a ninety-second audition piece. It's like hearing fragments instead of the speech. Have someone you know and trust listen to the audition material. Is it pause saturated? You might want two significant silences. Maybe three. Possibly four, but in most cases not more. Silence after silence destroys sense and is likely to make your work (sorry) boring. Weed the garden. Make the silences count. Silence should create meaning and tension, not destroy the fabric. Be disciplined.

THE DEAL

Allow me to level with you. I can tell you bunches of things that will improve your audition ten to twenty percent. I can tell you the generally accepted rules of auditioning. I can improve your flair and sense of presentation and how to catch the attention of your beleaguered auditors. BUT . . . unless you are good at acting's basics, it is likely to be all for naught. Let me remind you . . .

- Want something from the character you are talking to.

- Raise the stakes by making it crucial to your character to get it.

- Figure out what the obstacle is your getting it. No obstacle, no drama.

- Decide what tactics your character is using to circumvent this obstacle. If the text implies it isn't working, change the tactic.

- Be aware of your character's subtext. What's under and behind the words you are saying.

- Believe what you say. Mean what you say.

   These six things are the meat and potatoes both of acting

the play and doing your audition. Do them well and succeed. Do them badly and fail this eighty percent of getting the role. for the other twenty percent, read this book.

THE QUICK PART

There is particular way in which all auditions are all too much alike, rhythm. Most audition pieces are done at a moderate speed, neither slow nor fast, moderately loudly. Each line is likely to have considerable emphasis used so that each sentence sounds equally important. Frankly this is not going to get you the role. Somewhere in this monologue you need the quick part. Take the following two sentences.

"I never know what he is thinking. Yesterday he took a class in alligator wrestling."

Now when done as, "the quick part" you roll the two sentences together paying no attention to the period. Additionally you say it all very quickly (very) and without a lot of emphasis. Yes, try not to put more weight on one word than another. After two sentences, or a few, then return to your natural rhythm. This creates a wonderful dynamic, catches the attention of listener and makes for vibrant acting. Try it. It's like adding jalapeno peppers to a bland dish.

YOU CAN DO THIS

Here's the good news, you can do this, you can audition well. One of the reasons you can succeed is that the form is manageable in length. If you must perform two pieces, that is a total of three minutes of stage time. Now as a director I use the rule of thumb that each minute of stage time in a play needs one hour of rehearsal time to bring the work to an acceptable level (yes, I know, plays don't always get that but qualitatively it works for me). What I know you know is that good auditions are dependent on will power, you simply have to do the work. When the work has been done you need to harness that will power to do the necessary repetitions. Altogether I am suggesting a work/hour figure of six hours per piece, which includes both study time and work on your feet. I suggest that you shouldn't use a piece for an important audition that you haven't done at least two dozen times on your feet. Frankly, anything less than this simple regimen means you don't care enough to succeed.

CONCENTRATION

Auditioning presents every known obstacle to the laser like concentration needed for acting. We find ourselves in new surroundings, which distract and compromise the comfort in which concentration most easily arises. We're nervous, even frightened with unquiet minds. We feel no sense of creativity and are at the mercy of strangers. Where is the necessary concentration to come from? You are, to begin with, carefully prepared and armed with sufficient repetition. Remind yourself of that. Pick a point beyond those who listen to you and fix upon something real, a brick, a balcony rail, a stain, a lighting instrument and see it, really see it. Now add an image from the circumstances of the piece that you have already practiced. See in your imagination the waves roll in or the photograph of graduation on the imaginary wall. Breathe. Breathe again. Say the first line more slowly than you think is right. Include a brief pause in it. Take another breath and pause at the end of the first sentence. Look down and then up again. You will find you are now in the piece and concentrated. You will. Try it.

MUSCULAR PANIC

In dangerous situations our muscles tense, preparing for we know not what and the audition, in acting terms, qualifies as a dangerous situation. On the contrary our creativity as actors is dependent on having an impulse and following it and the tense state described above is creativities' obstacle. We want the realized state for our audition. Here's how. When you are about to be called in, stop talking to those around you or searching through your bag. Sit or stand relaxed but with good posture. Empty your mind as much as possible. Slightly slow your breathing. Will the tension from your shoulders, upper arms and lower back. Release your jaw, lightly flex your fingers. Feel your bodies weight relaxing downward. In your mind now walk through your childhood home while breathing regularly. If you need to close your eyes to enrich the imaginative trip, do so. When you are called to do your audition go in without hurrying. This is your time; take the extra seconds to make it so. Begin in a position particularly comfortable to you. You're fine.

PROFOUND SINCERITY

Auditions are made up of words and the weight of those words, their heft, their impact on the speaker gives work a gravitas that makes them powerful. Find a piece (or find in a scene) that allows the words to be crucial to the character who says them. This could be the case in a dramatic piece or a comic one. Whatever the genre these words should feel crucial to the speaker (the character). When I see an audition where the words seem unimportant to the character I come away unsatisfied. When you begin, say to yourself, "I have got to say this. It is crucial to say this at this moment!" This profound sincerity makes any actor beautiful and your short time on stage or film hard to forget and hard-to-forget results in casting. If you pick speeches that are really interludes in the text, which aren't the real deal, that which must be said, they are not a must for me to hear. Look for the moment of crisis or illumination. Casting will follow.

THE EYES

This primarily is a film, television and commercial acting note but certainly won't hurt you on the stage. Also this note will give many acting teachers coronary arrest so don't tell. In media the eyes are primarily the gestural, emotional and intellectual instrument. Period. No argument. You probably don't know very much about what your eyes can do and reveal. Go practice in the mirror (warning: I never said that!) Here's a start, say each of the following five things to yourself then let your eyes react in the mirror.

My God, he's been hit by a car.

Don't leave me, I love you.

You're going to think this is hysterically funny.

I'm going to kill you.

That's the cutest puppy I ever saw.

Now assuming number two didn't turn out exactly like number four and five you're beginning to see both your range and your limitations. Try another five. Get to know what *your* eyes can do. Now say the text of the commercial you're auditioning for and watch your eyes in the mirror. Say the T.V. side, watch your eyes. Kill em' with your eyes. But don't tell anybody I suggested such an old school exercise.

AUDITION ZEN

Seriously, the biggest problem in auditions is being scared to death of them. Don't live your fear. Look outward not inward.

Find a newspaper article that reminds you there is more

to life than acting. Carry it with you, and reread it while you're waiting.

Notice where you are. What color are the walls in the waiting room? How would you describe the actor across from you?

Remind yourself of four or five things you need to do today. Concentrate for a moment on how you're going to get them done. Project in a practical way beyond the audition.

Accept your nerves. Everyone has them. They don't mean much. They don't define you.

Challenge yourself to itemize what all the people are wearing in the audition room. Take a moment to write down what they're wearing when you come out.

In other words, be aware of the details of the experience. It calms you and gives you perspective.

AUDITIONING WITH STRONG CHOICES

Here's a surprising thing about auditioning professionally that I find most young actors don't know. As a director, I don't usually end up with several good choices. Usually only one person really stands out for a role—on a rare occasion, two. That means if you make strong, clear choices in your audition, you have a chance. Most people play it safe. When your powerful choice isn't what they are looking for, you may go down in flames. But, on the other hand, it may catapult you into contention. Don't be afraid to take chances. Base your strong choice deeply in the circumstances. Get your body into the scene. Let them see you think on your feet. Then go for broke. Your greatest competitive edge is the other auditioners' timidity. At the very least, it will mark you as an actor to keep an eye on. Don't just say the lines intelligently—want something desperately as the character and show it. Strong choices, obviously, are deduced from the text!

The Secret

Want to know what single audition failing is present in every actor I *don't* cast? They play every line in the same rhythm and often on the same musical note. This happens when an actor avoids deciding which lines are textually and situationally important by making all lines important. You see, if you were locked in a windowless room for eight hours (most audition rooms are, as you remember, windowless), would you want to pass the time listening to a metronome on one setting? Sometimes it actually feels like that. Thought has rhythms. Speech you would like to listen to has rhythms. Various rhythms. I've seen auditions that were all loud, all soft, all fast, or all slow, and I didn't cast a single one of those actors. The best acting is like watching a fire or listening to jazz. It isn't watching a obelisk or listening to a flatline buzz. Don't emphasize everything, don't yell everything, don't maintain a staccato. Please.

Be Clear, Be Simple, Don't Seek to Overwhelm

That's it. That's the audition tip. After all these years of auditioning, I have to admit I get mighty tired of the over-acting. I take it as a warning sign that the actor lacks taste, and to get a good performance from an actor whose taste is questionable is incredibly labor intensive for the director. We avoid such Herculean tasks when we can. An experienced director can measure your technique and emotional range without your making a fireworks display of it. Now, I'm not advising you speak quietly in a monotone—but reveal the role, don't carve it like Mount Rushmore. Make clear logic of what's being said (if it is logic). Allow the emotion to exist; don't wring it like a mop. Remember your auditors are probably (usually) intelligent and sensitive; don't spell it out as if to a child. If they like your work but are interested if you can enlarge, impassion, or double the ferocity, they will usually ask. I'm not saying work smaller; I'm just saying choose your spots for big.

AUDITION NOTATION

You come in; they hand you the sides (portions of the script to read) and say they'll see you in fifteen minutes. What to do? Whip our your colored pencils and make the following notations.

- Underline in red what you feel are the most important lines.

- Put slash marks (/) where there are transitions to be made.

- Circle key words you want to hit in blue.

- Lightly mark through in yellow the lines you want to throw away.

- Mark pauses you want to take with this symbol (V) in blue.

Now you could make up a dozen more marks for louder, softer, laugh, and so on, but keep it simple; you're an actor not a cryptographer. This takes practice. Pick up a book of audition pieces. Give yourself limited time to mark one, and then get up and do it. Don't try this at a real audition until you've practiced at least a dozen times. Then go for it.

READ THE PLAY

Sometimes you find yourself giving audition advice that seems so obvious you feel simpleminded. How, one might ask, could you possibly impress with the scene if you haven't read the play? For instance, it might help to know that the person you're beating up is your brother! Doesn't everybody read the play? No. I came from a set of callbacks today, and I'd say 20 percent hadn't troubled to peruse the text. Why not? Well, often there's a bit of trouble involved. You might have to travel to someone's office to get one or visit a bookstore to find one. Sometimes it's a new play, and you would have to sit in the waiting room and read it. Allow me to say that the odds against being cast become, well, astronomical when you don't know the shape of the role. Whatever you have to do to get hold of that script, do it. Even if it didn't make you information-challenged to overlook this detail, it would still make the auditioners feel you don't really care. Believe me, we want you to care.

AUDITIONING
FROM THE
SCRIPT

READING FOR THE ROLE

At a certain point in your career your auditions transform from doing a monologue to reading from the script to get the part. This is true in stage, film, TV, and other media. It may happen to you occasionally when you're eighteen but it's almost all you do at twenty-eight. It takes somewhat different skills. You may have a day or a week before the audition. You may get the script from your agent, from the casting director or from the bookstore. For stage work you may be given as many as a dozen "sides" to look over (and they may only have you audition one or two!) in film and TV and commercials it may be as little as two lines or the whole script. If you get a callback you know the lines but usually still carry the script. You will work with a reader (good or hopeless) who will feed you the other lines. In the room may be the director, the casting director, the producer, reps from the corporation or one lonely assistant. Or all of them. You may be in the room three minutes (commercials) or ten minutes (the stage). You are expected to give a performance, they don't care that you got the script yesterday. You may be one of 35 auditioners (stage) or up to 500 (commercials). The following tips give you . . . well . . . some tips.

HANDLING THE SCRIPT IN AN AUDITION

All right, your auditioning for Rosalind in Shakespeare's *As You Like It*. You've been given three scenes to look at. Now, what's the best way to handle the reading? Best of all, of course, would be to know the lines cold, but should you fail in that particular, I suggest the following: know the first three or four lines Rosalind has in each provided scene and, additionally know the last couple. This gives you a chance to actually act and be away from the script completely. You are holding the script, of course, and you have carefully placed your thumb at the point in the text where you will pick up reading when you reach the end of your learned lines. That way there will be no clumsy searching for your next line. Train yourself (practice, practice, practice) so that when you glance down at the script you can learn an entire sentence in a split second and can look away from the script as you act it (you'll be amazed at how quickly you can pick up this technique.) you can't do it with long and/or complex sentences and those you do have to be looking at the book. Now, and this is key, try not to be looking at this script while the audition's reader plays the other parts. This allows us to see you and enjoy your reactions. Yes, react to the other person because your sensitivity to what is said to your character often defines your audition. Don't simply act, *re*act.

SIDES

The text you are given for an audition to prepare and deliver.

Theatre: A side is usually a page (or two) of the script. Sometimes you will have been given many sides to prepare at a callback another two or three may be added. Though you have prepared several sides you may only be asked to read a couple. You just never know. Keep your sides with you during the audition even if you know the lines.

Film: Most scenes are one page long. At a screening audition they may only have you read one. At callbacks you may need to prepare several.

T.V. Series: At callbacks you may read a number of pages.

Commercials: You may be given one line of the full commercial.

THE READER

One of the hero's of our story. Really. If you are reading for a specific role in a play rather than doing a general audition there will be a reader. This reader (sometimes there are two, male and female) will sit facing more or less upstage with his or her back to your auditors and will read any and all other character besides yours to assist you. A sometimes overlooked fact is that the reader is human. If you treat the reader nicely and civilly and learn his/her name, the reader will work harder for you and a good reader, sensitive to what you are doing, and themselves a good actor, will make your work better. An excellent reader and an excellent actor are like a superb dance team working together. When you enter you may be introduced to those in the room. If not, it's a sure sign that it is (lovely term) a cattle call. If the reader is not introduced make your own introduction. If you have been given several sides (scenes) the reader will often point out which is which and the one usually started with. If the reader has the first line they will usually look at you until you nod or give some other sign you are ready. The reader will act the scene as well as possible so as to give you something interesting to work with. You, of course, may move around. The reader always maintains their seated position. When you are finished you say thank you to your auditors and thank you to the reader whose name you have been careful to note. Sometimes when you have left the room the reader will be asked her/his opinion of you. If you have been thoughtless, cold or ignore the reader . . . bad idea.

ACTING WITH THE READER (STAGE)

Play to the reader most of the time, not dead front to the auditors. When people do play endlessly front as if the lines were magically coming from somewhere other than where they are coming from, it often occurs to me that I should call a psychiatrist. Do not physically abuse the reader. Do not slap him, push him, hit him, kiss him or commit other forms of aggression or wild sexuality not listed here. If you find it necessary to touch the reader during your work, ask them if you may beforehand. If, say, there is a slap listed in the script, slap your own hand no closer than a foot away. If you have a special need as in, "would you mind yelling at me when you say, 'because I can't stand you!'" ask this acting favor before you begin. Sometimes the auditioning actor will ask the reader to leave their chair and join them onstage. I usually find this quite a bad idea because the reader feels self-conscious, even embarrassed and that quality can affect the work and spoil yours. Often the actor reading with you is playing the opposite sex. Simply play the scene, don't make jokes about it. Pay attention to what the reader is giving you in the scene and work with it. If you want a special quality ask for it at the top as in "I'd love it if you were really angry with me." Do not direct the reader during the scene, huh-uh, no way, absolutely not. (Handling the reader nicely is a sign to your auditors that you will be a pleasure in the rehearsal room and that counts big-time.) — *same w/ an accompanist*

COLD READING

The question is, do you have over night, or do you have ten minutes to prepare? For the sake of argument, I'm going to say you have an hour.

If there's someone around, ask him for a quick précis of the whole script. If he is knowledgeable, ask for any info on your character. (Obviously, this is outside the audition room.)

- Read the assigned scenes quickly, at least twice, for content, story, and meaning *without* making acting decisions.

- Underline key moments, sentences, and words.

- Determine what the character wants.

- Determine what the character's expectations are in the scene.

- Underline, in a different color, the major transitions.

- Learn, if humanly possible, the first two lines and the last two lines.

- Read it out loud at least three times trying different attacks and seeing where you can look away from the script.

- Play for one or two big moments. Play for one or two big problems.

  When you do it, do it!

REALLY COLD READING

"Read this for us." Can I take it outside? "No, just read it for us now." Gulp.

- Take thirty seconds to scan the page. If there's a long speech, glance over it—it will usually tell you what the major content of what you are reading is.

- Hold the script below face level; they want to see you.

- Run your thumb down the page as you read so you'll always know where you are.

- Hit the first line with strong energy and strong emphasis. Same with the last line! *Doing, frame it!*

- As you read the script, take a couple of pauses and during them memorize the shortest lines on the page so you can look off the text. Yes, it's possible.

- If you're not being videotaped, move a little. It will build your confidence.

✗ • If you make a mistake, don't look rueful, don't apologize, don't ask if you can go back. <u>Keep going</u>.

• Use emphasis. Don't read flat.

• Take an attitude toward the character and go full out.

• Look as if you're enjoying it!

Just try something don't go neutral.

AUDITIONING
FOR
SCHOOLS

WHAT IS A SCHOOL LOOKING FOR?

You are about to audition for a performing arts high school, a college theatre program, or a pre-professional graduate school of acting. What are these folks looking for? They, of course, would say "talent." What on earth does that mean? It means that in your audition they discern the following instincts present, which they hope to build on with their training.

- They want to see that you understand the material you perform and give that understanding shape in your performance. In other words, what's this piece really about? Is it about self-loathing or about your mother's attempts to discipline you unwisely?

- They want to see if you have a knack for believing what you say.

- They want to know if you actually have a thought process when you perform.

- They want to see if your body responds to what you think? Are your mind and your emotions expressed physically?

- Do you have the beginnings of a voice we would want to listen to for two hours?

- Do you have the energy to make material interesting?

They don't expect you to excel in all six areas but three or four reassure them that the training they provide will benefit you.

AUDITIONING FOR THE PERFORMING ARTS HIGH SCHOOL

In reality, you need one good piece. You should probably concentrate on contemporary work rather than Shakespeare or other classics. Why? It's easier to succeed. I suggest using a piece collected in this book because they have performance notes attached which will help you shape and deliver a good piece of work. Always use a piece that you feel is within three to five years of your age range. Acting forty- and fifty-year-olds obviously doesn't play to your strengths. As this is the beginning of your acting training you needn't feel pressure to be "Fabulous." You need only fulfill the following basics:

- Think, don't just talk. Set a couple of pauses that you do every time. You pause to decide what to say or how to say it.

- Don't rush. Rushing obscures thought and makes you seem frightened.

- Have some simple blocking to add physical component. Start out standing in front of a chair. A bit later move behind the chair and put both hands on it. Finally move in front of the chair and sit. Finish sitting. Something that simple. Don't wander back and forth.

- Make sure you are heard. Care about what you are saying. Don't use a lot of false emotion. Do the above four things and they will be impressed. That's plenty. Make sure you do the piece at least twenty-five times before the audition. Seriously. If you sing, show them. Performing arts schools love musical theatre talent.

AUDITIONING FOR A COLLEGE THEATER PROGRAM

What college program? If it's Julliard or Carnegie Mellon or North Carolina School of the Arts that's one thing. They are seeing hundreds of people and taking what they consider to be young actors in the top 5% of the talent available. They are, in fact, boot camps for the profession. If they don't take you it doesn't mean you have a lesser talent. It just means there is a veil of inexperience or actor-fear obscuring your talent. It's very common. These schools are a wonderful credit and give you first-rate training. Go for it. But there are other good programs, dozens of them.

Here's what your audition needs to show: the beginnings of an ability to handle and enjoy heightened language. That's why they are looking at your Shakespeare and that's why you must, must, understand every word and meaning, and mean what you say. Put all your energy into making the speech clear as crystal. You don't need a lot of movement. Deliver meaning and care about what you're saying. That will be plenty. Your contemporary monologue should be mainly dramatic. In this situation leave, silly comedy alone. They are looking for emotional connection.

Choose a speech, which expresses something about your own life. It has to strike close enough to home that you are not just saying something, you are expressing something. This piece needs to animate your heart and your body. It has to move you—literally. It grabs you and explodes you out of your chair. While the Shakespeare reveals your mind this piece reveals physicality. Remember, they are not looking for a completely finished performance, they are looking for a trainable talent. You can give them that.

AUDITIONING FOR GRAD SCHOOL

At last count there was at least eighty graduate programs in acting. Some take sixteen people a year and some take as few as six every two years. Most are three year programs, some are two and there are a couple of ones. Entrance (as far as I know) to all these programs is competitive. Auditions are scheduled in February and March in Chicago, New York and San Francisco, and Los Angeles. Some schools will also audition you on their campus. You usually need two contemporary and two classical pieces prepared. In callbacks they may also do improvisational, physical and vocal exercises with you. The top schools will see as many as eight hundreds applicants before picking next year's class. Some give the student little or no financial aid tuition support; some may give a full ride. They tend (though not exclusively) to prefer actors twenty-three and older. Some students in graduate schools are in their thirties . . . please remember these auditions are competitive. You can audition more than once for a school. There is always next year.

Some schools with good reputations in 2015 were Julliard, Yale, ART (Harvard), University of California at San Diego, University of Washington, University of North Carolina, Rutgers University, University of Tennessee, Trinity Rep., Columbia University (NYC) UCLA, USC, University of California at Irvine, and A.C.T. in San Francisco. However, this all changes as faculty changes. Don't take an offer at a school you haven't visited. Good luck. Use the web to check out programs.

CALL BACKS

THE TRIUMPH OF THE CALL BACK

Listen, enjoy your victories, and the callback is definitely one of them. It means that you were preferred over 85% (totally unspecific number) of your colleagues or, more simply, they liked you a lot. If you were in New York and had an agent (and getting an agent is another victory) and the agent sends you out to audition eight times and you were called back three times, that agent would think you were a very worthwhile property, even if you never booked a job. People who get callbacks have been noticed by the director, who will call you in again next time and watch you with great interest. You have separated yourself from the madding crowd and should go celebrate with a cream soda or a chocolate covered almond. I know, I know, you didn't get the part, but life is long and having your talent noticed is crucial. The next time that director does a play you may be at the top of their mental list because in certain ways you were *better* than the person he/she gave that last part to but you weren't tall enough, or you were too tall or you were perfect but you reminded her/him of his/her dry cleaner who she/he can't stand. So give a triumph it's due. You just did very, very, very, very well.

CALL BACKS

They obviously liked your work so keep it that way. Be careful what you change, including your clothes.

The changes you do make, make for clarity. The clarity of your intention. Clarity of the structure of the scene or speech.

* Come in with the lines learned. They want to see what you do when you're not tied to reading the text.

* If they have added a new scene (or "side") to your work, wonder why? What is this scene structured to "show"

91

about the character that the others did not? Then make damn sure this new element is given focus and that you embrace the new material.

- At the beginning of the callback it is fair to ask if there is a scene order that they prefer among those given?

- Deepen your concentration. Where does each scene take place? Does the circumstance of place add new acting details? Just one or two, retain the work they liked.

you can ask.

So ask

- If they told you in the first audition you would be called back, it's fair to ask if there is something special they would like to see? If they say, for instance, "a greater sense of danger," make sure it's there in the callback.

- Start and finish with scenes you are pretty sure you did well.

- Work the audition until you are sure there is no element of "audition fear" left.

- Bring your body to the work. Vocally use more than one rhythm.

You got a callback. Let them see you enjoy it.

you get to play one more time

STUFF

MAY I USE PROPS?

I love the fact that so many of the profession's rules are enshrined in a oral tradition! The basic answer is, depending on whom you ask, is sort-of, more or less, (well, there are some exceptions) no. The result of the community wisdom is that most people don't. Part of it is time constraint because people are being seen on a tight schedule. I once saw someone bring in a card table and a picnic basket full of silverware and glasses and arrange a table setting for four before starting to audition. This, of course, led us to believe she was mad as a hatter. No, she didn't get the role. I also saw someone bring in a dead pigeon to assist her audition for the seagull. Not good. My personal rule of thumb is that I don't mind common objects you might have in your pocket or purse being used. Car keys, a lipstick, a letter, a pencil, that sort of thing is fine. You could sort through your backpack, come up with an apple and eat it during the scene and I don't give it a second thought. When it gets more elaborate and specific or great in number it's just distracting and unhelpful. The audition is about you, not the material world. Some people would give you a flat no on any props at all so basically don't mess with them unless it's crucial to you. Don't bring in a blender and make a smoothie.

DRESS UP

No, don't show up in 18th century drag. It just makes you look desperate and of questionable taste. The trick is to dress *toward* the role but not to *dress* the role. For women an ankle length dress will serve for royalty. For men it's even less specific. Jeans and a white t-shirt would do for *Hamlet* (and don't bring a sword. Weapons in the audition room are verboten). You get it. No Hawaiian shirt and swim suit for Iago. You want a feel of the thing but not the thing itself. Some things just make demands. A CEO? Yes, a suit. A country guy? Jeans. A courtesan? Something that shows a little skin without embarrassing you. On the other hand you shouldn't do a tuxedo or awards dress, it feels like too much. A good sense of street style? Helpful. Someone not taking good care of themselves? A modified mess, fine. Truly filthy? Huh-uh. A ballet dancer? Dance shoes but no tu-tu. The Cowardly Lion of Oz? don't go there. Act it. Beachwear? No. no nudity. If nudity is demanded for the audition, you will be told and then it's your choice whether to go. I once did a play that (in part) revolved around a character whose legs had been insured for 10 million. Yes, we needed to see the legs but some women wore jeans. Hmmmm? Give hints that show you understand the character in terms of dress. Don't be literal.

How Often Do Actors Get the Part?

This one comes with a story. I once knew an actor who kept the most extraordinary audition records in hope of narrowing the odds. He had dozens of thick black notebooks with the info attesting both to his rigor and his lengthy career. He could tell you what his odds were if he auditioned on a Wednesday before noon in October wearing a suit and a red tie. Really. He was possessed. I finally asked him if it had assisted his percentage of offers and he said yes it had, over the years, but it's also possible, "I just got better."

There are just too many variables including the level of talent involved. I did ask a dozen younger New York actors and then averaged their answers for you. This came to booking one job out of twenty-five auditions. While this is a certainly unscientific, it's a little comforting right? It does tell us we can't mourn every audition that doesn't result in a role.

Buck up and move on. I also conducted questionable surveys of young actors in high school and undergraduate college theatre programs. In high school the fifteen or so actors I quizzed said they had gotten three to four roles and in college, four to six. It is illogical to give in to depression or despair because you have a bad audition or even a bad year. You're going to get better and so will your audition technique. You might not have been cast because you are too short, too tall or because you remind the director of his first wife. You can't control anything, but the work and creativity you put into the audition. If you have done your work you have to let the chips fall where they may.

INFO

If after a couple of weeks I haven't heard yes or no (and I have no agent) may I contact them to find out my fate?

If they wanted you, they would call you. You may contact them but you probably won't like the answer.

STUFF YOU CAN'T CONTROL

You auditioned; you didn't get the part. Stop doubting yourself. Here are some very possible reason why you weren't cast.

- you look like the director's ex-wife.

- They prefer someone who comes dressed as the part.

- They didn't like you coming dressed as the part.

- The part was already cast.

- They want someone who has played it before.

- There aren't enough leads on your résumé.

- You haven't played enough comedy.

- They wanted a different look.

- They wanted a different voice.

- They loved you, but they took someone with more experience.

- You're too tall for your love interest.

- You're too short for your love interest.

- They like actors with more technique.

- They don't like actors with too much technique.

- They've been auditioning for eight hours and hate all actors.

    Don't take it personally.

Audition Follow-Up

You did the audition and The Guthrie didn't want you for Edmund in *King Lear.* Now what? Well, the good news is they know you now. Keep it that way. Send the artistic director, director, and casting agent cards thanking them for the audition. Wish them well on the project, and express your wish to be seen for other productions. Send off these thank-you's within one week of being seen. If the director gave you an adjustment, thank her for working with you. If you know you will be visiting Minneapolis in the fall, ask if you may show them some other work at that time.

Also make notes in your audition diary about who was in the room (be sure to listen if they introduce themselves to you), and jot down any pertinent information you gleaned during the audition. You may run into these people again in a different setting. Wouldn't it be nice to remember them?

TOTALLY RANDOM ADVICE

- If you are doing two pieces, put what you think is your best piece first.

- Get there 15 minutes before your appointment, they may be running ahead (but I doubt it) but not earlier, it will just make you nervous.

- Everybody knows auditions are a terrible way to select an actor so take them with a grain of salt.

- Don't do a new piece just to do a new piece. Old faithful is probably better.

- If you are reading for a particular role and they stop you early don't despair. Yes, maybe they didn't like you but maybe they liked you so much they don't need to see more (I've done that a good many times).

- The more you talk about an audition the worse you'll feel. Before and afterward.

- Always have at least a half dozen pictures and résumés with you. Do it.

- If you feel you are truly, definitely, absolutely, and irredeemably wrong for a role, don't audition for it.

- Look like you enjoy auditioning. Directors like to mistakenly believe auditions are a good thing.

- Eat after the audition not before it.

AUDITION DONT'S

- Don't talk endlessly about the strange thing that happened on the subway. They are on a schedule.

- Don't come in for the callback if you have no intention

of taking the part. It really pisses them off.

- Don't try to pay the director compliments you don't really mean. It makes you look manipulative.

- Don't do the whole audition sitting down. Show them you can move with intention.

- Don't bring lots of props or set a table for four. (Yes, I've seen that.)

✱ • Don't say, "I'll bet you don't remember me?" Just don't!   *take direction*

- When you are given an adjustment don't do the same thing you just did. (Yes, it happened to me twice today!)

- Don't be rude to, manhandle, or sexually assault the reader.

- Don't do the audition two feet from the director. Back off.

- Don't wear eccentric clothing. We wonder why.

Auditioning for the Camera

TELEVISION 1

By Andrew Tsao

As far as serious television and sitcoms, the typical audition for most actors will be for small "entry level" guest or supporting roles on an established show. The first audition is generally for a casting director, who then selects candidates (perhaps four or five) to send to the director and producers for another audition. These auditions can be in person or nowadays, submitted electronically. The key here, above and beyond understanding the story, the role and the action of the scene, is making a strong well informed and clear choice about the character that can stand out.

Remember that in series comedy, heightened sensibilities and attitudes count for a lot. So a distinctive "take" on a character goes a long way even with a few lines. That means that a fully dimensional character we can access quickly and easily is worth a great deal.

Finally it is important to "button" a scene with a defined moment: a look, a "take," meaning a beat where the character discovers something or "finishes" something.

Precision is crucial, timing is essential, the best comedic moment gets the role.

TELEVISION II

By Victor Talmadge

For years I would go into an audition for a television show, do my work and never be called back. Finally after a TV audition, a casting director friend pulled me aside and told me that even though she could tell I understood the material, and even though she thought I had some talent, I was approaching the audition as if I were acting in a film, or worse a play. The problem was that I was taking too long with the material. She reminded me that the story on TV is told in either sixty or thirty minutes (including commercials). I was not there to languish in each moment. My job was to help tell the story as clearly and briskly as possible. It was a simple enough adjustment and it paid off. I started booking work. Not only because I was helping tell the story with the pace intended but also because I was demonstrating to the director and/or producer that I knew the technique of auditioning for TV.

T.V. – The Lowdown III

Day Player
Under Five
Guest Star
Recurring Role
Series Regular

In the "day player" and "under five" categories you might be given a single line to say. You enter the room, stand at your mark and say the line. The only other person in the room may be the casting director or an assistant to the casting director or some other associate. This person will, if necessary, read with you. You'll be in and out in a jiffy. As "guest star" or "recurring role" or series regular there is more of a process. You may read with an associate who, if they like it, they will show to the casting director. You may then be called in to audition for the head of casting at the studio level (Disney casting, for example), perhaps with the director present. If you are on track to be a series regular there may also be producers and the writing team in the room. (As many as ten people!) You might go on to an audition with the studio head or VP and one or two of their key people. This could all happen in a week or could take as long as three. What's weird about these series regular auditions is that they are often held in fancy conference rooms with people sitting all around you! But you're not done yet, now it's on to the network level and in that room will be network executives, casting people, studio people, and the Showrunner (who oversees the quality of the series).

T.V. – The Lowdown IV

Now if you have made it to this level, you have some fans who want you to succeed. The casting director has been in the room with you and the producer and the writing team now sees you as a real possibility. Soooooo, before you go into the room with the studio heads, the Showrunner (the creative generating force for the series and its day to day executive) and the original casting director, maybe a writer or two will meet with you and give you more background for the role, character tips and even line readings. Now before this final audition for network a seven-year contract has been worked out with your agent – even though there's still competition. They don't want to be in the position of liking you and not being able to afford you. Often, though not always, at this level there may be a warmer atmosphere in the room including smiles and response. All you have to do now is do good work under pressure and not freak out! There's significant money on the table now but there's no point in specifying amounts as they will have changed by the time this book is published.

FILM

None of this will surprise you, I think. You're going to need to work small but keep the intensity, you are, in a sense, giving a performance but not performing. In this media the eyes are truly the windows of the soul. They will usually be shooting you from high waist up. Gesture is minimal to non-existent. You don't want to be making a lot of "faces." The person reading the scene with you is usually not an actor. It could be the casting director's assistant, a script person or simply someone from the office. Sound restrictive? It is. This is an arena where the most emotionally transparent actors thrive, thought process is king and simple directness and honesty are the order of the day. If you look at something, look at something real, don't pretend. Understate rather than overstate. Set yourself on the mark they provide and don't move from there. Resist any urge to "chew the scenery." Mean what you say. You might add one (and only one) touch to your thirty seconds in front of the camera. You might at some juncture look slightly up or slightly down; you might raise one hand and touch your face. That, my friends, is as extreme as it gets.

FILM II

If you have an agent you will get the audition material two to four days in advance. Without, for the moment, going into the various role categories (under five, day player, guest stars, recurring role etc.) I can give you some helpful information. In most cases, for smaller roles, they move you in and out very quickly. Sometimes you'll be in and out of the room in a single minute and you may have only two to four sentences to work with. If the casting director likes you she/he may give you "adjustments" (acting suggestions). Don't discuss them, do them. Dress toward the role. If it's a businessman wear your power suit; if it's a ranger, jeans and boots. There will be very little small talk. It will probably be far more brusque than a stage audition. You're in, you're out. Sometimes the casting director will not even look up from their computer or make eye contact. Don't worry, it's not you, it's the business.

Occasionally, in film, they won't release the script to you. You'll see it for the first time at the audition. There will likely be little or no response to your audition. Laughter is a rarity at this level. You must find a way to relax under the pressure and manage your nervous system.

FILM III

- Hang your scene on your partner's eyes.

- Pick the eye closest to the camera lens.

- Hit your mark. can't do it here probably can't do it elsewhere

- Screen Test: Challenging scene from script is chosen.

- Watch screen tests on *YouTube.*

- Stay calm—breathe.

- When you get a call, who's starring?

- Check them out on Internet Movie Data Base.

- If T.V., what network?

- Ask if full script is available at casting director's office?

- SAG rule that script must be available 24 hrs. prior to audition.

- You can also ask whether it's a "tape read" or whether you will be taped.

- Check script carefully, pages may be out of order.

- Remember you are seen listening reaching and thinking.

- If you are "framed" chest up it looks as if your partner is only an arm's length away. Play vocally at that level.

- If you are told to "bring it down" simply lower your volume, not your inner life.

- Don't decrease your physicality.

- Pay big attention to the given circumstances!

- Don't play beneath your intelligence.

- "What is my *problem* with the other character.

- The Solution to the problem is what you are fighting for.

- Take risks and have fun.

BEDTIME

By VC Heidereich

The best advice I ever received was this: we often think we need to adjust the size of our performances from playing a theatre or room to playing the distance from us to the camera. This is often a mistake. Though the camera may be only six-to-ten feet away, the image it is collecting is much closer. And the image that is played back will be much bigger. What I was told was to give the performance I would give for my partner were we in bed together. That's what I was told. Keep thinking, keep changing your thinking, be so honest that you are available at six inches.

THE EYELINE

By Victor Talmadge

When talking to someone, always set your eyeline (where you are looking) at his or her eye that is closest to the camera. The camera is your audience *not* the people in the studio. So adjust your volume accordingly. The more you adjust your voice to a low conversational volume, the more effective you will be.

For TV you are dealing with a much more condensed format than film. Therefore, keep your pace brisk. Take a minimum, if any pauses. For commercials, this format requires very quick strong choices about personality. Decide on *one* personality trait for your character and play that.

CASTING DIRECTORS

By Victor Talmadge

Many actors feel the most important professional relationship they can make is with a talent agent. I would beg to differ. The real power is with the casting directors. When producers want to cast a project, they hire casting directors to do so. The casting director will put the word out to agents that actors are needed for a project and only then will the agent submit actors for the audition. However, if a casting director already knows and likes the actor the CD often requests that the agent have that actor sent over. Being requested by a CD directly also strengthens the actor's caché with the agent. In fact, even without an agent actors get auditions *and* book jobs because of their relationship to a casting director. Send them thank you notes after an audition. Send then flowers if you book a role they are casting. Do whatever you can to build healthy relationships with as many CD's as possible. They are the people who help make careers.

CAMERA PREPARATION

By Janet Zarish

Record the other characters lines. We spend so much time memorizing our own lines, finding our own intention, finding our own way through our own separate journey, only to sit in front of a camera whose defining characteristic is capturing and revealing reaction—the mystery of thought. Reaction in the television and film is just as golden as action and yet we are tethered to an audition experience, which seldom allows us to interact. Don't act alone. Get just as accustomed to hearing the thoughts that trigger your thoughts so that no matter who reads with you—an actor who gives you something or a casting director who doesn't, you have empowered yourself to know how to receive and respond. Turn on the recorder and do the scene while washing dishes, making the bed, filing your nails. Know the whole scene inside and out. You are alive in silence as well as when you're speaking. Get yourself a free recording app and set yourself and your imagination free.

Supporting Roles in Film

By Robyn Cohen

In film, and with supporting roles in particular, type casting can be your friend; when you're the type that is, and when you've come prepared. For me personally "prepared" means being off-book, in character, and having made the fullest use of any pre-audition time to craft a performance that understands the material. Doing diligence on the part beforehand allows you to take adjustments, connect with the words and create a life-like improvisational feel to your scenes. The camera sees all: inside and out, so living the material truthfully, moment to moment, is paramount. Fill the homework gas-tank and the car will go. But there's no trusting the work if it hasn't been done.

ON THE DAY

By Robyn Cohen

In television auditions it's helpful to show them what you will see "on the day." Filming for television moves at lightning speed, and even on major network shows, there's often only time for a single take before moving on. Thus, don't hold back your performance in the audition room, or on set. You may only get one shot! Also, going in with a professional attitude, assured and prepared gives them a sense you'd be easy to work with under those time constraints. In the audition room you may have anywhere from one person watching you to upwards of twenty studio and network executives observing (for series—regular roles), so it's important to be ready for anything. Toward that end, it's useful to have figured out ways, means and whatever techniques work for you to manage those nerves. Confidence will often seal the deal.

SIZE

By Robyn Cohen

In commercial auditions, size matters! Four of five times, either the casting director, the assistant running the camera, or the director (at the call back level) will give you the note to "do less" or "go smaller." Commercial styles have changed. A myriad of film and television directors are crossing over into the commercial world, and they are taking their (single-camera-quirky-half-hour-comedy) T.V. styles with them. It's subtler stuff these days and not so much oversell. Also useful to know that in commercials, physical character traits such as hair length, color, body measurement facial structure etc. become deciding factors in winning jobs. So in this medium, if you don't book the spot and someone says, "it wasn't personal," it may actually be the truth. You're still doing a thirty-second scene and should live it out truthfully and with all your technique in play.

TAPE YOURSELF BEFORE YOU GO IN

By Jenny Mercein

Now that every one has easy access to a video camera on their phone, my advice is to use it. Tape yourself. You learn so much by watching yourself. It's the best tool there is. Are your eye lines in the right place? Are your eyebrows doing weird things? You'll see right away if your work is too big. You can be your own director. You'll see on tape how small your acting can be and still be effective; also, purely technical, practice saying your lines without blinking. Watch film and TV, they don't blink. Don't lock your eyes as if it's a staring contest and it may feel odd at first but eventually you'll be able to do it without thinking about it.

ONCE YOU BOOK THE ROLE/ON SET ADVICE FOR FILM

By Jenny Mercein

Be courteous and kind to everyone. If you are rude to the craft services kid, it could get back to the producer. Be professional and be on time. Memorize your lines and know your lines cold. The old "hurry up and wait" adage is generally true but don't bank on having extra time for memorization. Be flexible, you may arrive on the set to find "new pages" waiting for you in your trailer. A set invariably has tons of distractions, especially if you are shooting outdoors. Even after "quiet on the set!" there's still a ton going on in your peripheral vision. You are just a small cog in a huge machine (lights, sound, background actors, etc.) you don't want to be the one who causes the director to call "cut!" because you forgot your line.

Being Off Book for On Camera Auditions

By Jenny Mercein

Yes, for film and TV auditions you should come in 100% off book. However, "on-camera" messing up a few words is far more acceptable than in the theater. Paraphrasing a bit if it enables you to truly connect to the material is better than just nailing the words in a disconnected or robotic manner. A bit of improv on the tag of a scene to show you understand the character and situation is usually ok. Of course there is an exception to every rule. You should always do your homework as to who is going to be in the room. For example, it is not a good idea to improve or futz with the words with an Aaron Sorkin script.

The Commercial Waiting Room

By Jenny Mercein

Commercials audition waiting rooms can be crowded and chaotic. Since commercials are often about a very specific "look" get used to sitting on a bench with six women or men who look exactly like you. For legal reasons you very seldom get commercial sides in advance. Arrive early to prepare. Sometimes the sides will only be a storyboard telling the idea of the commercial or they will just want you to tell a story about yourself. It's an unpredictable process. Even if given sides you have more room to improve than with film or TV. That being said, don't try to do a stand up routine. Almost all commercials now are very real and subtle. You will rarely have a "reader" in a commercial audition you may be paired with another actor, or read with the casting director or camera operator. Don't expect to get much help or "direction." Commercial casting folks can be stingy with the laughs. Don't take it seriously.

COMMERCIALS

- Never joke about the commercial or especially the product. Never. Never ever.

- Feature the product's name in your read.

- Dress the part.

- Have more than one read prepared. They may ask you for another one.

- If you are alone play the camera not the reader.

- Don't look down.

- There may be a storyboard in the reception area or the filming room. Look at it carefully; it may give you crucial context.

- Most often they are looking for your personality not your characterization.

- You will probably have thirty-seconds or less in front of the camera. Prepare.

- If the lines you are to say lack context, you may ask them for it before you slate.

- To "slate" is to say your name and the name of your agent, sometimes they will also want your height or other simple but pertinent information.

- If the room seems friendly you might ask to do a different read. They may even ask you do to so.

- They may take a still of you smiling before you slate.

- Know the lines. If you have problems there are cue cards.

- They may see as many as five hundred actors. Less than ten will be recommended to the next level.

- Steady on. It may be a while before you book.

AUDITIONING
FOR
MUSICALS

THE INITIAL AUDITION

By Gail Springer

At the initial audition I am looking for actors who are comfortable enough to communicate while singing, and so therefore have a personal, emotional connection to the lyrics of the song. I also want to imagine you inhabiting the world of this play. Select a song that is in the same style as the songs in the musical and adapt your voice, posture and gestures to suit that imaginary place. If the musical is *Oklahoma*, create an outdoor environment; if it's *How to Succeed in Business* dress and move as though you work and move in an urban corporate environment. Finally I want to know there's potential for us to work well together, so though your focus should not be on me during your audition, do look me in the eye and speak honestly and with positive energy during your introduction and in any personal interaction.

THE CALL BACK

By Gail Springer

At the "call back" or second audition, I'm looking for three things: character traits specific to the characters in the musical I'm casting, actors who respond freely to my direction and actors who listen to each other. During the time you are given to prepare the "call back," learn the songs or sides you've been given and make initial choices about the character's intention (or objective). If you read, or sing with someone else, listen and watch for what they are playing so you can adjust and respond to them in the moment with your voice and body. Be familiar with other characters in your range, because I may ask you to read Joan once I hear you read Mary. The quicker and more differently you can read or sing as the new character, the more versatile and willing I know you are.

Accompanists

By Steve Woolf

Like auditioning for a straight play, the first requirement is the simplest: know the story of the musical. Next, try to find out if you should sing a song from the show or sing other material. Not everyone can afford this, but you do yourself a service by bringing your own accompanist. That way it's someone you have worked with on the piece and you can't be thrown by some mediocre work at the keyboard. The piano player in the room will welcome the break. Don't expect transpositions on the spot and make sure the sheet music is easy to turn. Too much time in conversation at the piano leads the casting people to figure you will waste time in rehearsal or the song is too complicated for easy reading which speaks to a bad choice of material. Be sure you have several choices of songs so you don't get flustered when asked for another choice of song, or style of song during the audition.

Your Musical Book

By Heidi Kettering

The book is so important. First of all, always bring it. Even if you are going to a callback with sides. Bring your book. You never know when they will ask you to sing from it. Make sure you can sing everything in there. Sounds obvious, but time passes, and certain songs you could sing well—or that were appropriate for you—no longer fit that bill. If it's in there and the director says, "Oh, I love that song! Please sing that!" you don't want to say, "oh actually . . ." Make sure the music is clearly copied, the edges are cut off and that your margins are clear. Don't leave things to chance. The lovely accompanist may be amazing but they are not mind readers. Help them help you.

118

* "The Book" is your folder of music for auditions. It contains songs in many styles, ranges, cuts, keys—all of which the actress/actor can sing from memory. Mine is a black spiral notebook in clear plastic pages.

THE SONG

By Heidi Kettering

What are the lyrics of your song? What are you saying? Yes, sounding amazing is what we all want in an audition, but sometimes nerves get in the way, sometimes a cold gets in the way. But there is one constant . . . the words on the page. Tell the story. Use your techniques in singing too, but tell the story. Most of the time those notes are high and hard and scary because they suit what you are SAYING. That emotion behind the truth might just help you belt out that D.

YOUR CLOTHES

By Heidi Kettering

Are you auditioning for *Little Women*? Perhaps don't wear flip flops. Are you auditioning for the Beggar Woman in *Sweeney Todd*? Perhaps don't wear an evening gown. I don't necessarily feel you need to dress in costume, but for many reasons dressing as close as possible to the character in the show as you can is a good thing. First of all, don't make the director work too hard to actually see you in the role. Secondly—help yourself; you stand differently in heels than you do in cowboy boots.

The Five

By Deb Monk

Know what you are auditioning for. I'm always surprised when actors do not know the material or show. See the show, read the script, listen to the CD, go to *iTunes* or *YouTube* to see performances. Last resort, call the casting office with questions.

Know your character's vocal range! If you have to belt a high C and you don't have it you are wasting the creative team's time. Sing the song in keys that are comfortable.

Bring music. Have what they've asked for. Always bring extra music transposed in your key. Prepare several up-tempo songs and ballads.

If they are asking for a dancer who sings be that and a singer who dances. They will see what you can and can't do.

Be ready for scene work. Know who you are, whom you are talking to, where you've come from and what you want. Make specific choices!

THE ACTING BASICS
FOR
AUDITIONS

THE AUDITIONER'S "CIRCUMSTANCES"

Auditions need detail. Circumstances give you details to act. It's cold: you could zip up your jacket, stomp your feet and pull your sleeves over your hands. It takes place in a restaurant: you could signal a waiter, glace at a menu, speak a little louder because of the noise level. You're one of seven people invited to an execution: you speak in subdued tones, you glance away from the condemned because it's hard to look, and you might even cover up your eyes. Find the circumstances of place and situation that will provide the details that make acting seem "real." Circumstances provide the actor with an interesting physical life as well as an internal one. What do the circumstances make you feel? The audition room may be featureless and sterile but your circumstance transforms it for those of us who watch you. And in case you didn't know, we're grateful!

THE AUDITIONER'S "ACTION"

Let's stay really simple here. The "action" is what the character wants, what the character's agenda is at each moment. Auditioners who actively and with high stakes "want" will blow those who don't off the stage and out of the film. Oh, sorry, that sounds a little like an action movie, right? But oh, how true it is. You don't just want to tell a story about your mother's 19 cats, you want to tell that story to explain to your boyfriend why you don't want the darling kitten he brought you. When the "want" is a pressing, present need it's more powerful. You have ninety-seconds to "want" in an audition so you best want it ferociously. A central character in a play or film will act many "wants" while in an audition piece there won't be more than three. Your first job with the selected piece is to define the wants, each with an active verb.

THE AUDITIONER'S "TACTICS"

All right, you're "wanting" something all through the piece but how are you going to get it? You may be charming, you may be demanding, you may be flirtatious, you may be dangerous, all in service of the "want" which in this case is the last serving of a corn squash. So, once more, the tactic is the way you go about getting the "want." An audition piece may really only contain one want but you might use three very different tactics in ninety seconds. The "want" focuses the piece but the tactics give it variety. The tactic is chosen by the character because he/she feels it will work with this other person. The tactic is chosen with the other character in mind. Wanting something from your boss would probably entail a different tactic than wanting something from your sister. The "want" provides the drive the tactic provides the coloration.

THE AUDITIONER'S "SUBTEXT"

In certain circumstances, "I love you" can mean:
But not very much.
This is the last time I'll see you.
You are incredibly funny.
But I need a sandwich.

Obviously things we say don't mean the literal. The sub-text under the words often makes the audition juicy and memorable. I don't need to tell you to read the whole play, but in the reading look for the reasons that will allow your audition to have more than one level. Surprise us with the feelings under the language. There should be at least three rich subtexts in every ninety-second piece and even more in a read scene whether for stage or film. We love the actor who has a touch of mystery about them and that mystery is often provided by the subtext. Subtext comes from situation. What is the situation that surrounds the text you will be doing? Situation, situation, situation . . . Even more so in auditioning than real estate.

124

DIRECTED AUDITIONS

WHY THE 'DIRECTED' AUDITION?

For many of us the audition is a dangerously lonely process. We have no one to ask our questions of, or worse, we have the wrong person. What I think you need is a way in to the material. You need an experienced person to give you a few ideas to get you out of the starting blocks. All advice is flawed, however advice based on substantial experience gained at high levels of the profession is worth considering, even if you eventually reject it. This is a way to bat ideas around when you have no such partner available. There are your ideas and my ideas and out of bumping them up against each other will come a third idea (a better idea). Thus, it's my pleasure to work with you on your audition. Pick a piece and let's get at it.

JANE AUSTEN'S SHOES

Woman:

Shhh, shhh,. This is something you can't tell . . . ever. Ever, ever, ever. I'm wearing Jane Austen's shoes. On my feet. Cross my heart. My great, great, great grandfather... actually I'm not sure how many greats but . . . but he slept with Jane Austen. Really! He was a, you know, brick-fixer, brick-putter inner, layer . . . that's it. Odd that should be the word, but he was . . . fixing . . . and she invited him in for tea and she attacked him. Like a tigress. And, I don't know how to put this, they did it in the parlor. She scared him to death. And then she fainted and he thought it had killed her! So he ran. Never went back. And somehow he had her shoes in his hand. Jane Austen's shoes. They've been passed down. I have them. And you know what? I wear them whenever I serve tea.

(*She moves downstage*)

And on other occasions we won't speak of.

Performance Notes:

Play it like a secret conversation that mustn't be overheard. What she is telling is a big, amazing secret. Find a couple of places to look around you to make sure you aren't overheard.

When you get to, "But he slept with Jane Austen." Spread the words "But … he – slept – with – Jane Austen."

During the "brick-fixer" sentence really struggle to find the right word. Let there be some inner confusion.

She's a little shocked by what she has to tell so "They did it in the parlor" is a shocking revelation.

The monologue can be played sitting or standing but if sitting you should rise on "and then she fainted and he thought it had killed her." If standing, move downstage on that line.

" . . . he had her shoes in his hand." Hold up arms as if holding the pair of shoes by the straps.

"Jane Austen's shoes." A little delighted victory dance.

"I wear them whenever I serve tea." The subtext is: isn't that amazing!

SOFT DRINKS

Man or Woman

Hi. I'm back. You look a little stunned. Don't apologize, I completely understand it. I go out for ginger ale and I'm gone two years. The problem is there isn't exactly an explanation. I went to the Food Mart over on Euclid and they only had 7 Up so I drove out to the Seven Eleven but they were closed, so I kept going because there's that all night Shell station but they were out and I kept going and suddenly it was thirty-six hours later and I was in Florida. But see I couldn't explain why I was in Florida so I couldn't call and then I saw the signs to an airport and I ditched the car and caught a flight to Milan and it just kind of went on from there. But last week I was on a beach in Indonesia and it hit me that I really wanted ginger ale so I figured the Shell station would be restocked so I came back. I know that doesn't make any rational sense but it's as close as I can come. I guess the question is: Do you still love me?

Performance Notes:

Define your relationship and feelings toward the other character as this is clearly a relationship piece. The other character could be family, a lover or even a dog. Each choice would change the acting. This piece confronts some of the mysteries in living a life. Why do we do what we do? Our character clearly isn't sure, and this lack of surety, this confusion informs the acting. There is the quality of "figuring out" here, he/she doesn't exactly know "why" but does know he/she wants to be loved. That makes the last line the most important and the actor must find a way to do so. The character does not feel in control of life and realizes that instinct not rationality is driving them. The acting needs to capture how this situation is working itself out. This done, the piece will have a special impact.

LIFE COACH

Woman:

Hi, I would be your life coach, Adrianna. Yes, I'm young, I anticipate your question. But youth has answers. Youth knows. You are older so your insight is cluttered up with too many experiences. I'm fresh; I'm like a piece of really fresh fruit. I can still see the forest for the trees because I don't have a lot of trees yet. So, this being our first meeting I would say to you . . . sit down and shut up! Good. Here's how we fix your life. Clean up your damn house! This is like hoarding only all the stuff's expensive. Throw out two of three objects. Walk around. Out, out save. Out, out, save. Then! Kill your sister. Your sister is a bitch. At the very least, smack her around. Finally, kiss the first ten people you meet. And I mean *kiss* them with a capital *K*. Do these three things and I'll se you next Wednesday; and get my check in the mail, girl! With a 20% tip for insight. Here's an extra—you dress creepy, get a tank top. See you Wednesday.

Performance Notes:

Adrianna, is confident, she speaks crisply. She has probably said many of these things before. On the other hand, she's nice and she has a sense of humor. She's firm but pretty charming. She's not obnoxious.

She is speaking to a client in her late twenties or early thirties. She thinks of this client as a contemporary not an older person. Adriana is probably twenty or twenty-one. She's been telling people what to do since she was seven and most people enjoy it and enjoy her.

She is making a house call. She looks at the stuff around her. She looks behind her. Sometimes she leans in and whispers.

She has gestures (which she repeats) for "out, out, save."

She checks her watch before "do these things and I'll see you next Wednesday." She claps twice before "and get my check in the mail, girl!" she smiles when she says, "you dress creepy, get a tank top." She waves goodbye on "see you Wednesday."

Take a pause to look around before, "this is like hoarding . . ."

Adrianna is, in some sections, well . . . cute. Something darker plays on "kill your sister . . ." then she recovers before, "at the very least smack her around."

She's a little lonely, not vicious. The crucial thing is to stay likable.

WHO YOU?

Man or Woman:

This is really hard. This is harder than I thought. If I could get it I would want forgiveness in advance. The thing is, I don't love you. Please, I have to finish. I thought you were somebody else and you turned out not to be that person and I thought I would be somebody else with you and it turned out I was meaner-spirited and less forgiving than I thought I would be. So in a sense it was just the self I imagined getting together with the self you imagined and neither of us have really been there. And I realized at Christmas that you gave presents to a person I wasn't and I think what real lovers do is give the right present, a present that's recognizable as an insight to the person who gets it. So all this just means that our love had to miss each other like trains on different tracks. We invented each other and then we fell in love with ourselves. So that's why I cleaned out the apartment. I wanted to wait to tell you and now I have. Bye.

Performance Notes:

This piece would benefit from simple activity such as putting on and tying your shoes, or doing your lipstick or getting a sliver out of your hand, etc. this might go on until, "and I realized at Christmas . . ." then you should allow yourself some stillness until "we invented each other." When you would rise. The final line is a move away toward an exit with a turn back for, "Bye."

The speech isn't accusatory. You are just trying to tell the truth as you see it without being mean-spirited.

A key line is "so all this just means that our love had to miss each other like trains on different tracks." Make it stronger vocally and more emphatic.

Pick two or three sentences where you aren't focused on telling the other person. On those lines you are realizing something on the instant.

The end is meant to be an awkward moment. The character doesn't know how to end this conversation and does so clumsily.

The final word, "bye" is tinged with regret.

EMOTIONALLY DENSE

Man or Woman:

Don't you even think about saying that. No! Quiet! I don't talk about my emotions?! That's just . . . I can't . . . how bloody dare you? If I talked about my emotions . . . my emotions!?. . . I would be screaming at you in the drugstore or we would be rolling around in a fury in the WalMart parking lot. You drive me crazy! And that's not an emotion it's a medical analysis. The only way I manage to put up with you, your hoarding of Styrofoam cups, your fourteen hour videogame debauches, your lack of any discernable style and the incredible noises your body makes, is to keep my emotions in a locked box, in a vault, in my windowless heart surrounded by armed Amazons and protected by my murderous rage. No . . . wait . . . I do have an emotion I want to share which I hope will satisfy your longing and that emotion is . . . leave me alone!

Performance Notes:

When playing people in extended rage (and she/he is in rage) you need to be concerned with variety. Shouting for a full minute and half probably isn't employable or enjoyable. In this piece you do need to start high and the character is on an emotional roll. You can probably rage your heart out from the top. Through "and that's not an emotion it's a medical analysis." At that point take a pause to calm yourself down. When you start again with "the only way I manage to put up with you . . ." be measured even calm but with your anger still underneath it. This dangerous calm remains all the way through " . . . protected by my murderous rage." The final lines the anger starts to break through again, finishing with an enraged (and probably loud) "leave me alone!"

You should have some acting fun in this rage. Kick over the chair. Throw your shoulder bag or backpack against the wall, kick the door. You are allowed to excess as long as the middle is calm.

132

She/he *hates* those Styrofoam cups.

When she speaks of her emotions being kept in a locked box she is explaining something to him he has probably never understood.

You shouldn't play individual lines in this piece you should bundle the lines into several bunches with pauses in-between.

BUYING

Man or Woman:

Yeah, I only watch the commercials, I edit all the other stuff out and then I try to understand all the stuff we buy. Cars and insurance and shampoo and beer. So I guess that's who we are, right? If you have that stuff and do that stuff then you're satisfied and life's good and you hang out until you're dead. You ever feel empty, Jake? Ever feel like you're the victim of some enormous tasteless joke? I mean, what exactly is lite beer? Why is it we need four hundred horsepower? What the hell, if you don't mind me asking is AFLAC? Are you happy? I'm not happy. I think my life is, most of all, an example of buyer's remorse. What exactly happens to a life overwhelmed with a lack of meaning? Now if I were to analyze the two of us, I would call us glazed, drugged, clinically without feeling. Oh, there's the Adidas ad. That is so cool. I'm cool. You're cool. Shoes are cool. Maybe it's time to go to bed.

Performance Notes:

This one could start lying on the floor or leaning against the audition room wall smoking weed (mimed, okay?)

The performer is a little laid back and a little pissed off. Maybe it's late at night. Maybe the other character has been trying on some stuff purchased that day. I believe the speaker is not in his own apartment and knows the other person but not well.

For the first few sentences don't talk directly to the other person in the room. Talk to the ceiling, talk to your left foot.

Don't relate directly until the line, "you ever feel empty, Jake?" the section after that should have a quick driving pace through " . . . AFLAC?" then pause, then "are you happy?"

Play "buyer's remorse" like a big fat movie title.

When he talks about "a life overwhelmed by lack of meaning." He is grimly taking about himself.

None of the television downstage catches his eye. He stares at it. After "shoes are cool." He watches the T.V. in silence for several seconds. Then he says the last line as he walks directly upstage and, supposedly, out of the apartment.

Beaches

Man or Woman:

No, I don't actually want to lie down on the pearly sand, in the glorious sun, after immersion in the turquoise waters of the pristine Caribbean, Lucy. I am not a hedonist; I'm a namby-pamby intellectual as you well know. I come to the beach to find shade and read fully dressed. That's me, take me or leave me. And no, I don't like fun. The fun I see you all having seems to me to be resolutely devoid of fun. Let me run this down for you. You painfully burn your skin lying in the sun in a bikini that is a catastrophic mistake, run into uncomfortably freezing water and then lie down and get sand all over yourself and you dare to call that fun? And, oh, while you do this you eat hotdogs. Hotdogs! The food God forgot. Spare me, oh Funmeister. Let me take my Tolstoy to the cleft in the rock and leave my sunless, funless, sense of deprived life. And while I'm up, can I get you a diet coke?

Performance Notes:

I'd start this sitting on the floor reading a paperback version of one of Shakespeare's plays. Yes, I'd have that prop. I would keep the book in front of my face for that first long sentence. Then I'd lower it to say, "I am not a hedonist, etc."

On "The fun I see you all having" I would get up and brush sand off myself.

Now I would be as charming as possible and starting with "You painfully burn your skin, etc." I would tick these off on my fingers. It's a list.

He is horrified by hotdogs. Be horrified.

"Let me take my Tolstoy to a cleft in the rock etc." Don't over theatricalize this. Be logical.

On the final line take sunglasses out of your pocket and put them on.

He's with friends who understand his crotchets.

He's not too bitchy and he's having a good time doing this.

WINGED FEET

Man:

Bike messenger. I know, I know, inconsequential. My parents are embarrassed and my brother says I should get, as he so delightfully puts it, a real job. Thanks Marty, really glad to hear your opinion, bro. But, but . . . I am becoming the god. Mercury. Laugh, go ahead. He showed up about a month ago, started running along beside me, which is pretty weird in Midtown. He wants to retire. He's had it with Olympus. Don't ask. I AM NOT JOKING!! I'm the chosen one. I'm going to replace the god, Mercury. I have feathers growing out of my heels. I can now ride a bike seventy miles an hour, up hill. The point is, I'm going to have to break the lease. I'm apologizing, sell what you can. I can't take my stuff to Olympus. There is no stuff on Olympus. I go Wednesday. I don't know, I don't know, I feel like I have to say yes to godhood. Finally my brother will be impressed. Oh, oh. Feet want to go. Can't say no to the feet. Really you'll have no problem renting. Oh, oh. Adios.

Performance Notes:

Situation: the character has just gone down to his apartment's rental office to tell them he is moving out. The rental office is looking at his file and said, "Your job is what?"

The style is very conversational. He knows his story is hard to believe but by now he has had to tell it several times—to his family, to his employer etc. Something out of the ordinary and wildly hard to believe is happening to him but it is happening. He is beginning to get extremely irritated at not being believed.

He explodes on "I am not joking."

He tries to be completely logical and dispassionate on the "I am the chosen one" section.

When he speaks about Olympus he has been there in the very real dreams he's been having.

As he starts "I feel like I have to say yes" his feet force him to run in place (against his will!). They move faster and faster during the final dialogue until they literally run him off stage.

Keep remembering what it's like not to be believed when you are telling the truth.

FIRST DATE

Man or Woman:

Okay, I know this is just a first date but I feel I have to come clean because I have this problem of speaking in really long sentences because in fourth grade I had this teacher, Mrs. Tupolac, who was obsessed with criticizing my punctuation so to avoid humiliation in the classroom I started, well, dropping punctuation wherever possible thus keeping Mrs. Tupolac off my back but creating a conversational style which is a little one-sided because as you will shortly notice there is no way for you to respond or participate as there are no interior pauses ordinarily created by sentence structure, which has had a really negative effect on my romantic life and created the impression that I am a narcissist totally disinterested in others whereas in actual fact I find you really attractive and, I'm sure, interesting, if it were only possible for me to shut up but as I don't seem able to accomplish that I wonder if you would mind helping me out here before the entree arrives by stopping what is happening here with a kiss. Ah!

Performance Notes:

First of all, we have to recognize that this is an audition piece that is also a single sentence. As the sentence is too long to do on a single breath, we have to take a series of quick shallow breaths so that it seems the piece never stops until just before, "ah!"

This also affects the emphasis because emphasis uses up breath and here we are trying to conserve it. Here's what you do. You're going to have to create a breath score which you memorize in the same sense that you memorize the words. In other words, you will breathe in exactly the same place every time! You can use commas for a quick breath. You can use connectives such as "and," "but," "or" for the breath. The technique is to hit it hard, create a tiny pause for breath and then go on.

The situation is that this person really, really is interested and attracted to the person they are talking to. They would desperately like to shut up but cannot. You can punish yourself for this fault by hitting yourself but it doesn't work. Gestures are good. On "I" you indicate yourself and on "you" you indicate the other. You can agonize on "really negative effect on my romantic life."

In the nice solid pause before, "ah!" close your eyes and slightly purse your lips. Hold that for say, three seconds then open your eyes and say "ah!" and smile.

Guys

Woman:

Yo. Ummm. Could we, ummm, turn off the mother-loving, endlessly repetitive, totally uninvolving, ummmm, sports? Because, Jackson . . . can you hear me, Jackson? Jackson, is your brain receiving information from other humans? Jackson!! Politics exists, religion, science, literature, crossword puzzles, even, and let me emphasize, making love. Love, Jackson, eros can be as absorbing, under certain circumstances, God forgive me, as basketball. Really. Read my lips. I need love, Jackson, don't you? Because how many ways . . . how many . . . can a ball be put in a basket? I watch these games with you and nothing, nothing changes but the color of the uniforms. Nothing! And I need the warmth of lips, the shape of hips, the texture of skin, the electricity of the forbidden and all I am getting, Jackson, is zone defense. Turn off the game!

Performance Notes:

It's been a long evening for our heroine. She thought she was being taken out for dinner but instead he took her to his place (or family home) so he could watch the game and all she has had to eat are some stale chips and murderously hot salsa. He is completely absorbed in the game. She sits. The room is overheated. He's cute but this is ridiculous. She's been out with him before . . . to a game. Finally she went outside to get some air. She came back. She's not happy.

When she starts he's not listening. She's trying to be pleasant. The "Jackson!!" explodes out of her. She didn't realize that was going to happen. She has shocked herself. She tries charming him. She kneels in front of him for "read my lips." She slightly loses control again on " . . . can a ball be put in a basket?" He doesn't respond. She looks at the TV in silence for 4 or 5 seconds. Next she tries to entice him through " . . . zone defense." Nothing. Quite loudly she says the last line spreading each word "turn-off-the-game."

Note: As to "entice him" it needs to be charming rather than so heavy handed it turns us off.

ANOTHER WAY

Man or Woman:

Yeah, right, I can put it another way. You remember when Peter Pan tries to sew his shadow back on? We read Peter Pan 'til I was like nauseous. Well that's what I'm doing here; that's why I want the money for an MBA, so my shadow will finally be long enough to satisfy you. To for once, one time, satisfy you. Wasn't the valedictorian, oh-oh, shadow got shorter. Didn't make the Ivy League, oh-oh, didn't go to law school, fell in love with a hairdresser—oh, oh and oh, oh. So to cast the shadow you always wanted I want the MBA because then, finally then, you might be ready to see me and not my shadow, and that would really mean something, it really would. There's a difference between doing and being, Pop, so take a look at the being or give me the money for the doing. Please. Please.

Performance Notes:

The character, Man or Woman, is talking to their father and this relationship is obviously troubled. This is a conversation that has been a long time coming. What is at issue is not only respect, but money. We might imagine that our character has come to his/her father for money to support a graduate degree and father is not convinced. In all, a troubled, difficult conversation.

Think of the piece as a combination of anger and pleading. When it begins, the character who has probably been overemotional has been asked to "calm down and put it another way." As an actor that gives you a chance to start with a barely enforced cool or calm. From there the piece gradually accumulates anger and then quiets down and becomes the pleading I mentioned before.

The heart of the piece is the character's deep need for approval from a parent. There is deep sincerity in the line " . . . and that would really mean something, it really would." Make sure the piece is not only about anger but about love. Also make sure the final two words, "Please. Please." have two different qualities.

WORD

Man or Woman:

Hey. Hi. So, I'm auditioning for you today but I have this problem with honesty, blame my mother, thus in the interest of full disclosure I have to tell you that I'm not as good as this is going to look. Why, do you ask me? I have spent at least two hours a day on these pieces for six months and it's probably the case that I will never, never spend that long on two minutes of stage time again. I wouldn't spend that long on *King Lear*. So, the point is, this doesn't represent the general quality of my work which is significantly lower. Plus, let's get this all out, we flew in my coach who teaches audition at Julliard. So, if you take me into your program, you will be getting what I think they call a pig in the poke and you will be surprised and disappointed by just how much I ordinarily suck. On the other hand if you view acting's primary needs as "truth" and "honesty" then you will be honor bound to accept me. All right, let's get going, my first piece is . . .

Performance Notes:

You want laughs? This piece will get laughs. It also is a tiny bit risky and close to the bone but that just gives it a dangerous charm. What's needed here is kind of ferocious sincerity. This is like George Washington and the cherry tree. This character cannot stop himself/herself from telling the truth. There's a compulsive quality to it that you want to find as an actor. You can even take a couple of pauses trying to stop yourself, but the truth will out.

Remember, he is not apologizing, he is doing full disclosure against his better judgment. (When played by a woman, the play *King Lear* should be changed to *Hedda Gabler*.) There should be a significant pause after "I wouldn't spend this long on *King Lear.*" He knows he is now going to say something irredeemably damaging to himself. He tries to stop but . . . he finally decides he has gone so far he cannot go back.

At the end he tries to redeem himself with optimism. He smiles. He is hopeful. Maybe he's just done a good thing.

Keep it conversational. No theatrical extremes. The subtext it, "I know I shouldn't be saying this but my mother is out there watching me."

ONE A.M.

Woman:

Get out of my face! I am seriously telling you to back the hell off! Do it! Now! Not only do I have no, zero, nada desire to kiss you but I find you unbelievably, hopelessly, irredeemably revolting and why I came out here with you to the middle of nowhere when I knew perfectly well what you had in mind, I can't even fathom! So let me make this perfectly clear, I am not going to end up the night as another notch on your revolver and a story you tell at halftime over a beer. That is not going to happen! Back off! That's better. Now it is obvious you are smart, you are talented and I admire your shoes but other than that the gods have not favored you. So if you would kindly put your pants back on we can drive back into town in a merciful silence that will be prelude to never speaking or spending time again. If it will be of any help to you, please view me as insane. Now put the key in the ignition!

Performance Notes:

Start out high and hard and don't pull it down until after, " . . . what you had in mind I can't even fathom!" she then calms down but with iron in her voice until she explodes again with "This is not going to happen! Back off!"

After "Back off!" he obviously does. She now adopts the tone of an indulgent mother explaining to a five year old that he cannot eat his shoes. Then a final explosion on "Now put the key in the ignition."

This is not a hysteric speaking; this is a strong woman whose red-line has been crossed. She is not afraid; she is in charge. When she says "why I came out here with you to the middle of nowhere when I knew perfectly well what you had in mind, I can't even fathom!" she hates having had such bad judgment. It has never happened before.

The guy she is with probably had some prestige. Quarterback or somebody who had gotten on a reality show. Going out with him wasn't attraction it was about gaining prestige. It was stupid and she hates being stupid.

BLUE MOON

Man or Woman:

My father was a crooner. You know what that was? Silky voice. Sang twenty-three different songs about the moon. You know who Frank Sinatra was? My father covered about two hundred of his songs in about two hundred hotel lounges in all fifty states every year. So we would see him about once a month whenever the gig ended. He would usually pull up to the house about three in the morning with a dozen red roses in one hand and a bottle of gin in the other. You know what gin is? So he would stand on the lawn singing this really satin version of a song called "Blue Moon" and Mom, Carrie, Mort and I would open our windows and applaud. Sometimes he sang in the snow, sometimes he sang in the rain but he always sang when he came home. So, I never really knew him and now I never will, but I miss him. Sometimes I have to hum "Blue Moon" to myself to go to sleep.

Performance Notes:

So we've all been in this situation, right? Or if you haven't been you will be. Give yourself a few years. Your parent (mother or father) had disappointed you, made you wildly angry and not returned to you. You have every reason to hate this parent but instead you find yourself missing her or even becoming more like her. This monologue is a case in point. You're talking to your new best friend or love-to-come who has told you, admiringly, about his/her parents. You start your story almost unwillingly; you don't want to get into this. You do get into it and soon you like telling it . . . it's a good story. And then you run into the hard part . . . he basically abandoned the family. You feel some unreasoning guilt about it, almost as if it was your fault. Perhaps you've never told anyone this whole of this before. " . . . but I miss him." Is a new discovery for you. You never fully realized that before. The final sentence is an intimate revelation. It's almost embarrassing to be this frank with someone you don't know too well. Then you can't go on. Perhaps you start to say something else and then don't. The piece is over.

THE PROPOSAL

Man or Woman:

Look, whoa, stop for a minute, okay? This stand of oak, we came past this? See the two that are down over there. Okay, this scares me. Last light and as far as I can tell, we're walking in circles. I'm not . . . don't get edgy, I'm not, you know, attacking your . . . woodsmanship, you're very cool, cool but what I say is possible, right? Don't walk off on me! Sorry, sorry, nerves. I don't have a coat; we don't have matches, no sleeping bags. This could be pretty bad, right? Below freezing. So I would like you to get over yourself and talk this over. I don't think you should keep walking fifteen yards ahead of me as if I didn't exist because I would prefer not to freeze to death. Are you listening to me? Hey! Don't leave me here. All right, fine, I'll marry you! Oh, now you turn around. Very romantic. You actually know where we are, right? This isn't funny! No, I don't retract the question. Are we on or not? That's wonderful! Now, where are we?

Performance Notes:

This is a piece full of misdirection. We think it's one thing and find out it's another. Play it like that. The speaker, obviously upset, is trying to stay cool and failing. The person, he or she, is speaking to is the nominal leader of this expedition but seems to have failed in the clutch. The speaker still needs the listener, so they are trying to be cool and calm but a little hysteria leaks through. Now under this seeming situation there is another we don't find out about until the last moments. The speaker has been proposed to but either surprised or unsure has not given an answer. In these last moments the speaker loses the last vestiges of control when he/she agrees to marry. To really make this work, the control must not be lost earlier. The final two lines are polar opposites. "That's wonderful," is romantic elation but "Now where are we?" is truly worried. Make absolutely sure these last two lines embody two entirely different feelings. In the midst of this emotional battlefield find a couple of sentences of the calm the speaker wishes he had. Opposites make this piece work.

The Honeymoon

Man:

I give up. No, I quit. I'm done. We're on our honeymoon and you've won seven straight games of Monopoly. I don't think that's what the pastor meant by holy matrimony. If you have more Monopoly games than you have sex—or as the pastor puts it – cuddle-duddling, then I don't think we call it connubial bliss, I think we have to call it . . . Bullshit! Sorry, sorry, I know you don't like me to take the bull's name in vain. C'mon, that's a joke! Just trying to lighten the mood. What is the problem here? I love you. I love you way more than Monopoly and I would like to express that love outside the parameters of Solitaire, Risk, Ping-Pong and beer pong. Oh, oh, I know a game. Let's take each other's clothes off with our teeth. We each have three minutes and . . . no, it's a real game. Oh yeah. We can figure out how to keep score. You're smiling! Okay, ready? One, two, three go. Go! No, I don't want to discuss the rules!

Performance Notes:

Ah, the tension of two inexperienced, or perhaps just very, very nervous, humans on a honeymoon. The circumstances create our drama. He loves her, he wants to do all this at her speed but the conflict is he can't stand it anymore! It starts with an outburst that he immediately regrets. He calms himself but, can't avoid another outburst on " . . . Bullshit!" then realizing he's blowing it he tries to make a joke and that doesn't work. Underneath these emotions, he is truly worried. Finally, after " . . . Risk, Ping-Pong, and beer pong," he manages to get her to smile. This calms him and he is comfortably and charmingly in charge and finishes in laughing frustration with "No, I don't want to discuss the rules!" Remember that no matter how frustrated he gets he loves her. If he is simply angry and unpleasant the speech dissolves. We have to like him. When he says "I love you" we absolutely have to believe him.

PICASSO

Woman:

No, very clear. Your comments on the paper are specific and helpful as always. You've changed my way of seeing and I didn't know, didn't project that, as a benefit in an art history class. Thank you. But one thing . . . you just touched my hand Professor . . . I know it could be described as reassuring but we might also call it exploratory don't you think? Like your compliments for my earrings, remember those? And the way I'm singled out by . . . well, so many things . . . walking me down the hall after class. And these things could give the appearance of . . . well, I don't like to . . . don't need to say the words do I? My father always says that "chaos lies in wait" and I think that's true don't you? You need to . . . well, take care, Professor. We all do. So, thank you for your help with Picasso. I appreciate it. There's so much to learn from him. I look forward to the next class. No, I'll open the door. Enjoy your day.

Performance Notes:

Pleasant but no attempt to charm. Clear and concise. In control but unthreatened. These qualities will make the piece work. Nothing highly emotional, hurt or revengeful. This young woman knows precisely what she wants to accomplish. Where you see three dots as in " . . . well so many things . . ." a pause is useful. The nature of these pauses is so much like a chess player considering the next move. When there is a question mark actually ask. These questions are not meant to be rhetorical. She is even cheery on, "No I'll open the door" and "enjoy your day." She isn't dealing with a criminal. This is a teacher whose class she enjoys and wishes to continue enjoying. This is a well-considered preemptive strike to prevent something she sees coming. There is something measured about the way she does it.

THE SPIDER

Woman:

You killed the spider. It occurs to me you like to kill things. The robin that was hurt flying into the glass door, you drowned him in the rain barrel. Hunting season, you always love that, and it makes me wonder, idly, if I actually know you very well? Do I? Do you think I do? Because I keep thinking about that night in the summer . . . the incredibly humid one . . . when I woke and you were standing by the bed looking down at me. There was . . . a feeling . . . like something disturbing the air, something . . . well, the word might be ominous. Or not. I know it's stupid but . . . that's what I felt when you killed that spider . . . it made you a stranger, just for that minute . . . but . . . I don't think I'll stay here. Not tonight. I don't know exactly but I don't think I will. I'm sure it will pass. I'm sure I'll remember that I know you. Call me tomorrow if you feel like it. Oh, I made a pie. There's a pie in the fridge. I couldn't remember if you liked pie. Do you?

Performance Notes:

This is that moment (we've all had them) when we realize we don't know the person we're with as well as we thought we did. And that's disorienting, right? It's like the horror movies where someone you're eating dinner with begins to transform into a werewolf. This piece takes place in the middle of a conversation. She hasn't meant to get into this but something he says or does (killing a spider) opens the door for the way she is now perceiving him. It's important how this piece starts. Start with a pause in which you consider whether to say what's on your mind or not. Start slowly and build up steam until you get to the first set of dots. Now she slows down because she is telling him she actually feared for her life. When she says "I don't think I'll stay here," she decides that at that moment. As far as she's concerned the relationship is over in that instant. Then she remembers she made pie. It shocks her that everything felt so normal just an hour ago.

BUCKS

Man:

Three hundred and forty million and change. I got the ticket, number 384277865 and I'm nineteen. They don't know I got it yet. Nobody knows I have it except you. Is that cool or what?! My parents? They do okay. My sister Leah? Married in the suburbs. There's no real reason to share, y'know? Three hundred and forty million and I live on $1600 a month outside what Mom and Dad pick up. So what, you might ask, will I do? I'm thinking I'll buy a town and be the mayor. There's three, four towns available on Craig's List which is weird right? Not that I really want to move to Nebraska, but hey. And in this town I will have the best car, the best house, the best bar, and I will effectively be the king. Beneficent. Louis the Nebraska Fourteenth . . . me. I got small dreams, but I like power. What about you? I thought I might give somebody thirty, forty million just to watch the comedy. Tell you what, anybody who wants it raise your hand. Just kidding.

Performance Notes:

This is a direct address to the audience so they question arises, who are they? And the answer is simple, the audience. Or, if you prefer the people auditioning you. This gives you a chance to break the Golden Rule and address your auditors directly. Do it. He's known about the ticket for several days, maybe a week. He knows his life will change completely now. He knows his relationships with the people he mentions will never be the same. He's decided to shut them out. There's some anger under the speech, a slight feeling of revenge about to manifest itself. He has been powerless so his line " . . . but I like power" is an important moment to him. He already knows people will rise to the bait of using him and benefitting. He knows he can now manipulate others greed, his final line, "Just kidding" is cold as ice. He also likes the absurdity of buying a town. He's nineteen, working and not attending college. He wasn't living a life of possibilities and now these possibilities are limitless. He knows his listeners are riveted by his gigantic good fortune and he plays them. It should be a little scary.

Hey . . .

Man or Woman:

Jeez, I don't know, y'know, 'cause it's . . . y'know . . . I mean how . . . okay, okay, like I know what you're getting at . . . hey, you know I know . . . but uh, but uh . . . so it's what? It's uh . . . jeez, my watch . . . I musta . . . look, we're both on the same, y'know, and uh . . . you gotta watch on, right? You gotta watch on? So don't . . . awright, jeez, I get it you . . . keep your shirt on okay, because . . . awright let me put it this way . . . or . . . no this way because . . . could we pay a little attention, if you know what I mean . . . like eye to eye here . . . like uh, like uh . . . wham! Contact! So we uh, we can sort this . . . right? Right? You and me? Bam! Communication! Which is . . . which is . . . the words, y'know . . . you get it? The words, y'know . . . you get it? The words, whoosh . . . gone like socks under the bed, right? Hey, no problem, we uh . . . you and me, me and you, we got . . . whatamacallit . . . you get me, right. We uh, we uh, we understand each other, okay, right? Are we copasetic? Cool.

Performance Notes:

Usually in audition material we have to discover the reasoning, here we have to invent it. This might be an act of bullying in a hallway, or it might be someone admitting an attraction, or it might a warning delivered. You pick. Once you decide on the intent you need to know how each broken sentence would have been completed. Write the whole thing out making the broken sentences whole. It starts as if our speaker has been told something, "like I know what you're getting at" and proceeds to our speaker taking control and implying the listener knows how this will play out. Personally I think a threat has been delivered to the speaker and he lets the other person know he/she better look out. There's a sort of gang or mob overlay in the writing as in, "don't do what you are telling me you're going to do unless you want to end up in the river." The other key is to make sure your thought changes after each dot, dot, dot. This piece is written to show off your mercurial thought process. Make sure you do that.

PARASITE

Woman:

So, what's the big objection, right? I think I'm correct here that we agreed on this, or am I missing something, some detail here you would care to enlighten me? Oh, I get the look, right? You got a helluva lot of nerve, no kidding. I pay for your life, right? The drugs, the steaks, the couch you are at this moment sitting on, the whole boatload of your, so to speak, expenses. And how I do this is pole dancing at "The Crazy Horse." For me, despite the difficulties, I was at that time underage! Do you understand you piss me off with your scruples and this . . . this . . . what can we call this? Interrogation? I dance, that's all I do down there, then I maybe have a drink with my girlfriends and I come home. So, get-the-hell-off my back! I'm serious. You're like those fish that live off the shark, whatever they call them. You're a parasite is what you are. I'm done with this. Go get me a beer.

Performance Notes:

This human is already damaged when we meet her. She's angry, she's hurt and she's lashing out. Before she speaks she's been accused of infidelity by her boyfriend in the room with her. Whether she did it or not (you make the decision) it's the last straw for her. He also wants her to quit her job which she is responding to in the first few sentences. The first line she's already shouting. She pulls down to icy anger starting with "you've got a hell of a lot of nerve" through "your, so to speak, expenses." She takes a breath and tries to be logical rather than angry but unable to sustain it explodes again on "so, get the hell off my back!" her anger has exhausted her and she then speaks almost without inflection. Take a solid pause before the last line. She realizes now that she's gone too far, that she has no way to escape this guy and her job. The last line is softer, almost an apology. She's trapped.

MR. KREBS

Man:

Yeah, I'm a Marxist, what's it to you? Oh. I see that word is strange to you. It's not unusual. You must in no way be ashamed. My father had only three books. *The Bible*, which he said was the greatest fantasy ever written. *The Joy of Cooking*, which he said was the repository of all pleasures and *Das Kapital* which was the dawn of truth contained in two sentences; "the more the worker produces, the less he can consume; the more value he creates, the less value he has. Machines replace labor and jobs diminish while, the rich get richer." So that is why I can't work for you anymore Mr. Krebs, despite your kindness in giving me a summer job. Here in Butterworth, Kansas, you are the only capitalist swine available to me and I must strike a blow for labor. Please give my very best to your wife and my thanks to your daughter for the time she spent with me in the dumpster. There can be no social harmony while one class exploits another. I hope you'll come to the baseball game this Saturday, we've won three in a row.

Performance Notes:

This is a very smart kid and being smart has probably isolated him from his age group. He reads, he goes to the movies, he's very much alone. His only social activity is baseball though he spends most of the time on the bench. He has worked for almost a year in Mr. Kreb's hardware store. When there are no customers he sits and reads *Das Kapital* by Marx, which drives Mr. Krebs crazy. When the monologue begins Mr. Krebs has called him a communist and suggested he get off his butt and do some work in the stockroom. He starts with a tone of hurt dignity, and is attempting to take "the high road." On the moment he decides to quit although he needs the money. Finally his façade cracks and he is bitterly sarcastic when he speaks about his relationship with Krebs' daughter, the school Valedictorian. He was probably never in the dumpster with her. On the line "there can be no social harmony . . ." he is beginning to give a speech to the imaginary multitudes. He stops himself. He actually likes Mr. Krebs. He would really, really like him to come to the game.

SLEEPING BEAUTY

Woman:

So I was going down to India House to get some takeout and this, I don't know, gift shop, has this sign in the window that says "life is a special occasion" and I realized we don't have that together. We have constancy, habit, safe haven, a kind of general all purpose, predictable warmth but "occasion?" I don't think so. What are we doing in a relationship where we give each other socks and reference books for Christmas? This is only guesswork but I think a "'relationship" would be harder than this, more demanding, less habitual more . . . something. More damn something! Could we, for instance, have sex sometime other than Wednesdays? Really, I sometime think this is a case of our sitting around telling each other how warm we are, when there aren't any matches. I don't want the tombstone to read, "nothing ever happened!" Do something! Break something! Have an affair with my sister! I would actually like that, I'm not kidding. Kiss Sleeping Beauty and let's get this on the road. God, I'm bored!

Performance Notes:

This audition starts at a breaking point. She just cannot go any longer without saying this. She's decided it's time on her drive home from India House. He's sitting at his computer and she walks in and watches him for a moment. He says "hi" and she says "hi." He goes back to his computer and she starts in. Now, upset as she is, remember she still has a sense of humor. She still wants this relationship to work. The center of the piece and the line that needs to be different than any other is: "what are we doing in a relationship where we give each other socks and reference books for Christmas?" Nail that one. Also beware of playing this whole piece in one tonality. What she wants is assurance that he will address her concerns. To get that from him she needs to use more than one tactic. For instance, she might start out using logic, switch to anger, go on a humorous approach and close with "demanding." You need to decide what tactics she uses before performing the piece. You might also take a strong pause before the final line, "God, I'm bored."

ACRE STREET

Man or Woman:

I'm on the street because my mom, she asked me would I get her some mayonnaise 'cause my dad don't like no dry sandwich, so sure I'd go and my brother "little" he comes too, so my mom could get some peace and quiet. And we're down on Acre Street where it dead-heads on Parson Avenue and this Range Rover . . . silver Range Rover driver guy flips me off so "little" he flips him off back and the guy gets out of the car and shoots my brother dead. Shoots him through his blue left eye. Shooter, he smiles at me, says I should teach my brother some manners. Then he tosses a twenty on the ground like he was payin' for a six pack. So that's how my brother finished up. When he was thirteen. My mom still cryin'—cops didn't get nobody. My daddy he walks all day Saturday and Sunday lookin' for the Range Rover, says he's gonna fuck somebody up, but you never get revenge 'cause it don't work that way. You just grieve. That's your job. We all got the same job in my family. We grieve. That's what we do.

Performance Notes:

Can you do this believably? If so, this is a piece where you should shape your work backwards from the last lines "we grieve. That's what we do." The actor is talking about tragic events that occurred sometime ago. The wound is no longer fresh. Perhaps he is explaining his brother's death to someone he hasn't seen in a long time. Maybe he's drinking a soft drink or beer. What is still freshly painful is not his brother's death but it's effect on his parents. He still sees that (and feel it) everyday. You have to make acting choices about what is still painful to him in the piece and what he has come to terms with. Those two things sound differently. We also need to know his relationship to each parent. He might, for instance, be alienated from the father and still really emotionally close to his mother. The moment in the remembrance that is still connected to anger is, "shooter, he smiles at me and says I should teach my brother some manners." Other than that, anger doesn't play a big part in the piece.

SEVEN

Man or Woman:

So, I said, Dad for cryin' out loud, the seventh dwarf is Sleepy and he throws a glass against the wall and yells, "you can't have a seventh dwarf without a sixth dwarf and we only got five dwarfs, Doc, Grumpy, Snoozy, Bashful, Happy!" An my brother says "there is no Snoozy, quit counting Snoozy!" and mom say she thinks there's a "Creepy" and Dad flips out calling us all idiots and I say "Forget it, I'm going to my room." And Dad says "nobody leaves the room 'til we finish the dwarfs!" and my brother says "Yeah?" and my father says "yeah!" and my brother jumps out the bay window and there is glass everywhere, and my mother starts screaming we need a doctor and my father says "that's it, Doc! That's the seventh dwarf!" and my brother who is bleeding on the lawn says "we already got Doc, that's still five!" and my mother gets in the car, goes downtown and institutes a divorce. The dwarfs break up the family. Doc, Grumpy, Sneezy, Happy, Dopey, and the one nobody remembers! Who the hell is that seventh dwarf?! I can't afford to lose another parent.

Performance Notes:

Comedy, obviously. This piece is meant to be very much in the present moment. "mom" just filed for divorce yesterday or the day before. Both the wound and the emotional recall are fresh. Let's say, as a circumstance, that this character is responding freshly to something that happened yesterday afternoon and it's now the next evening at his/her weekly get together with friends. The speaker is stoked with anger and disbelief. When the piece starts the speaker is already a minute or two into the story and has momentum. I think this piece is best done in one gulp and the only significant pause is after "Doc, Grumpy, Sneezy, Happy, Dopey, Sleepy and the one nobody remembers!" at that moment the absurdity and frustration the character feels has peaked. Note the ex-clamation point. The next line "who the hell is the seventh dwarf?" is the real question the character wants a real answer to. The final will be, depending on what you feel is quieter, even reflective. The piece also begs for moments of wide-open physicality. Not all the time mind you but at two or three carefully chosen points.

EIGHT BALL

Man:

No more, Jimmy. I got a personal philosophy makes all that stuff irrelevant. You got way too many problems in your head you can't do a damn thing about. It's Friday night, you have here three friends from grade school playing a little pool for a few laughs and a couple beers and you're wasting this worrying about Iran and global warming and a bunch of brain dead Republicans? No, don't walk off! Tell me this, compadre, what precisely will you do about these things? You will do nothing. Nothing! You know it, Chuck knows it, Berry knows it and I, one hundred percent know it. You're the only one who doesn't know it! This makes you at best, moronic, pal. You become, at the Elm Street Bar and Grill, a figure of amusement. I'm telling you "don't sweat problems outside a three block radius." Plus, plus! I don't want to hear it! Now pick up your cue and be a screwed-up human being like the rest of us. Jeez! Gimme a beer.

Performance Notes:

Don't even think about doing "Eight Ball" if you're not entirely comfortable handling a working class persona. You have to know this guy to pull the piece off. He's not angry (irrational perhaps) but he also has a sense of humor underneath his mini-lectures. The second sentence, "I got a personal philosophy makes all that stuff irrelevant" is not paid off until very near the end with "don't sweat problems outside a three block radius." That line needs to pop in some way. It could be louder than other moments. It could be slower. It could be more emphatic. In any case it needs to imprint itself on the listeners brain. It's the line that defines the piece. At the beginning of the monologue the pool game he is playing with his friends has been stopped cold by Jimmy's long speech about the state of the world. "No more, Jimmy" has to stop Jimmy cold. When Jimmy walks off you need to follow him; it being one time you might seem to be actually angry. Remember, the basic tone is not threatening. There's a certain warmth because he's known Jimmy since grade school. Everybody at the table knows Jimmy tends to mouth off but hey, let's play some pool!

TOBY, TOBY

Woman:

Toby, Toby, Toby, I don't love you. I'm sorry Toby, Toby . . . I should love you. It would be only fair, right? You are loveable, everybody agrees on that. You're smart, you're mildly good looking, you remember birthdays, you're six foot one, and you dance. All of this Toby, Toby, puts you in a highly recommended category, really it does, but I have this horrible, undependable, lifelong problem, Toby, Toby. And that is, you are unfunny as a stone. You are. You only make me laugh because you're never funny. You do tell horrible unfunny jokes about hermaphrodites meeting parrots in bars but they freeze the room Toby, Toby. They are like a Minneapolis winter. I am begging you not to love me. But here you are. You keep showing up no matter how far from Pasadena I move. This is Thailand for God's sake Toby, Toby. What are you doing here?! The answer is no. I'm going to say it ten times. No, no, no, no, no, no, no, no, no. Okay, that's eleven. It's-not-going-to-happen! All of life is a joke, but you don't know the punch line. Stop grinning at me.

Performance Notes:

First of all, why is Toby's name always repeated? "Toby, Toby" is his nickname, his friends have called him that for years. Probably because he has a log of wild, impractical ideas and people were always shaking their heads and saying "Toby, Toby!" He has been in love with this woman for years but though he is a dear friend she's never been romantically interested. Now he has come to find her all the way in Thailand! She's had a tough time. Her marriage broke up, she had breast cancer and her employer sent her to work where no one else wanted to go. She is, secretly really pleased to see him but doesn't know what to do with him. Eventually they marry but she doesn't know that's her fate. It does drive her crazy that he has no apparent sense of humor. His lack of it is, well, funny. He has probably shown up at a difficult moment. Maybe she's been trying for two hours to pay a traffic ticket but nobody speaks enough English to handle it. This event with Toby takes place in public which makes it harder to deflect him. Every time she looks at him he's smiling so she tries not to look at him a lot. Just his being there finally makes her laugh. And yes, she goes out to dinner with him.

ATTRACTION

Man:

I lay women to waste. We're dealing in fact here, not wish fulfillment. They cannot get enough of me. It can be very difficult, even overwhelming. I frankly wouldn't wish it on you. I sometime fantasize about wearing riot gear. Joking, but . . . why, I ask am I such bird bait? Yes, I'm handsome . . . in a sort of unusual way. Yes, I'm funny without being vulgar. I do social commentary not bar jokes. As to charm, yeah, on a good day. But none of this explains the multitudes. I get stopped on the street and propositioned. My parents put bars on my bedroom window. I gave up my iPhone. I literally fear a gang of feral women will . . . I don't know . . . carry me off to their lair and . . . well, I don't go into that. I think of scarring myself but it's not just looks. I think I need to smell. I need to smell revoltingly. That's why I came to Rite-Aid. Can you recommend a product? No, don't touch me.

Performance Notes:

First of all, it doesn't matter how this guy looks. He is not conventionally handsome. Women just want him, he doesn't know why. For awhile that was cool but now he's trying to finish a graduate degree and working two jobs. He doesn't have time or energy. He just wants to be left alone and that isn't happening. He's embarrassed by the attention he gets. This guy is by no means a player. He is talking to a Rite-Aid employee who also happens to be a woman. She's fascinated by him, which is the last thing he wants. So, most importantly, he isn't proud of his ability to attract, it's sort of ruining his life. The key is, he needs help. The action is to get help with this embarrassing problem. There's a hunted quality about him, like a soldier behind enemy lines, he looks warily around him as if he might be attacked. "Can you recommend a product?" is filled with hope and longing. Remember this is a man fighting to survive.

PIE

Man or Woman:

There is literally nothing left to eat, Mother. I'm not talking about the refrigerator or the pantry. I'm talking about the world. There is no foodstuff left that doesn't have a downside as itemized in a hundred studies I don't want to know about. But you . . . you Mother will not leave me in peace. You subscribe to *Food Weekly, Organic Gardener, Raw Monthly, The Government Food Warning newsletter* and now this, *The Poisoned Dinner* and *Vegetarian Death Recipe's* and you read them to me, Mother . . . you follow me to the car reading them. I beg you . . . look, on my knees I beg you to stop this, because I do not want to know the tenuous link between broccoli and leprosy or buffalo burgers and "the dancing madness first observed in Strasbourg in 1518." You weigh under a hundred pounds. You're becoming translucent and you're taking me with you. All I ask is that you let me eat with you. All I ask is that you let me eat this pie with whipped cream. If my face rots so be it. Please.

Performance Notes:

This character has searched the pantry, the kitchen and the fridge for some food, any food, he/she would actually like to eat. The mother in question, sits there dispensing warnings on any and all goods chosen, and critiquing the choices. Finally she/he puts down whatever was chosen and maintaining a rational tone begins the piece. Our character loses his cool on " . . . you follow me to the car reading them." Underneath his irritation he is truly worried about his mother. He's been scared to tell her how unhealthy she looks. The final two lines are sweetly furious and the final "please" is the loudest moment in a basically quiet piece. The character is beginning to feel that he/she lives in a madhouse. He/she went on the scale this morning and discovered in horror that he had lost another five pounds. This is a piece where a character loving control tries desperately to stay rational and logical. That accomplished you can pick the single moment where the character loses it.

PAST TENSE

Man or Woman:

And I'm supposed to be glad your back, right? It's almost unbelievable, no, it is unbelievable. Terrific, my father cuts out two days before my birthday nine years ago and we get nothing, not an email or a postcard or any damn sign you're alive or even care what happened to Mom or Kenny or me and now you walk in with a smile and a present they obviously wrapped for you in the store. How impressive is that, or your life for that matter? Mom's out, in case your interested and Kenny might be in school, who knows? He's a mess, by the way, screwed by Vicodin, Xanax, Dexadrine and you. You, Dad. He totaled the junker you left us so we all used the bus 'til Mom won that car. Did you know she won a car? Not that I care, because that's the deal, we don't care anymore. This isn't, you jerk, damage you can repair. So I'm sorry because I loved you. I really loved you. Past tense. I don't want the present. Get off the porch before I call the police.

Performance Notes:

This character is a survivor, who in consistently hard circumstances has excelled in some way. You should pick something you've excelled at. Imagine she/he hasn't seen her father in nine years and here he is! And for nine years she/he has imagined what would be said. The harm the father has done the family comes flooding back. The current pain is Kenny's decline and drug use which is, I think, the angriest part of the piece. The most emotional moment is your telling the father you loved him. And loving him has made you even angrier at this obstacle. The speaker is obviously very protective of his mom. I think he/she wants to get rid of the father before the mother returns home which is imminent. The key moment in the line, "This isn't, you jerk, damage you can repair." You want to make sure the weight of this line lands. The final line is ice cold and an actual threat. The piece, for obvious reasons needs to take place standing in the doorway. No way is our character going to let the father in!

THE POOL

Man or Woman:

Yeah? Uh-huh. Uh-huh. Uh-huh. Oh I hear you, oh yeah. But where's the piece of paper that says I owe you? You got that piece of paper? See, the reason you don't is 'cause that piece of paper doesn't exist, not in this world, and unless you print up a paper like that out of your mind, then this lottery ticket . . . well, that would be my lottery ticket. That would be my 180 million, out of which, you pray hard enough I might send you a nickel, and that baby, is a definite maybe. See there's the lottery pool and there's a single only ticket I buy for myself alone which I got right here in my pocket gonna deliver me to the promised land. So, hey dudes, bring on the lawyers 'cause here's the truth, they ain't no proof! Y'all laughed at me, didn't keep me no place at lunch, hid my tools on me and the almighty brought down his retribution in the lottery, honey. Eat your hearts out. I've got and you've not. One hundred eighty million, baby. But you look out in the mail for the nickel, uh-huh. I'm gonna send that right along. Next week, the week after.

You can count on it. Send you a post card from the Bahamas. Come on down!

Performance Notes:

So, the situation is this; our character was part of a group at work who bought lottery tickets with the understanding that anyone who wins splits equally with the other buyers. However, the speaker has been consistently bullied and made fun of at work and now that he/she has won, has no plans to split the one hundred and eighty million. Unfortunately for the others the deal was never written down. It's a revenge piece and the speaker is enjoying the situation. This enjoyment is crucial to the acting. The monologue takes place on the factory floor where they all work just as lunch as commenced. There are probably eight to ten other workers involved. Our character will go directly out of this "meeting" upstairs to the office and quit forever. Find expansive moments such as " . . . deliver me to the promised land" and "I've got and you've not." He/she spreads his arms wide and looks up to the generous heavens! If you've got a good stage laugh you should find a place to use it. This character is so thrilled he's not even angry anymore. Oh, this is sweet revenge!

SLIVERS

Man or Woman:

No really, this is George Washington's finger. I mean this is supposed to be show and tell for American history, the colonial period, right? And, you know, I've been sitting here for the parade of candlesticks, and clay pipes and baskets and crap, realizing I have the showstopper. I mean what is better than a physical digit from the top guy? So, here's the deal, you all remember the story of George Washington chopping down the cherry tree and then manning up and taking the responsibility? Well, the kid had never handled an axe before and, whack! Off comes his pinkie and hey, he's screaming bloody murder! Out runs his mom, Mary Ball Washington, and she tried to sew it back on with her sampler needle but no luck, so she makes a tourniquet from her undies thus saving American independence. Pretty good, huh? The finger gets wrapped in a hankie and his dad, Augustine sticks it in a secret drawer of his gaming table which my grandfather bought at auction. Now if the class will line up, I'll shave off some slivers from the finger so everybody can have a little. Best Show and Tell ever, right?

Performance Notes:

You should have a prop for this one. Perhaps a marzipan finger (or even half a pencil) wrapped in a small cloth or Kleenex. Our character has left a classroom desk and made his/her way to the front of the class. Tattoo's and piercings and alternative dress set the stage for this one. You can also throw in a few "uh's" to characterize this monologue, but no more than four or five. There's something a little smug here. This character knows full well she's got the showstopper and she likes the attention. She also knows she'll shock the room by offering to cut off slices of the finger. Our character also loves the drama of the losing-finger-story. Play it with some relish! Close the piece with a sense (as the character) that you've done a great job.

FRUIT SALAD

Man:

Isabella? Ummm, Isabella could you get off your Mac for a minute. Isabella?! Is-a-bella!! Thanks . . . sorry. Listen . . . umm, sit over here, okay? Great. We have been, uhhh, you know, since uhhh, last summer but there's, well, this thing I haven't told you. No, it's not about prom night with Darleen . . . that was complete rumor. No truth at all. See, the thing is, ummm, I'm a superhero. This is not a joke, Isabella. Not a big time superhero, you know, not Wolverine or a superhero like that. Isabella, the truth is not everybody makes it. There are hundreds of loser superhero's and uh, well, we kinda keep it on the downlow because, uh, well the reality is, Isabella, we kind of suck. It's embarrassing. All right, so who I am is Plum-Man. Yeah. I can turn myself into all kinds of fruit. To tell you the truth it's both useless and dangerous. Blueberry-Man got eaten at a buffet in Chicago last week, like cannibalism. Oh boy. I had to reveal this, Isabella, because sometimes I turn purple during sex which might be a little scary for you. And all I'm saying here, is when there's fruit around, talk to it first, because it might be me.

Performance Notes:

Pure silliness, which is usually a nice relief for those judging auditions for three days. After Sophocles, Shakespeare, and Beckett, believe me, we are ready for a goof. The one thing to remember about comedy is that it's very, very serious. The character in "Fruit Salad" is very, very afraid of being eaten. He's also afraid Isabella will think he's crazy and he loves her. Yes, don't forget "Fruit Salad" is a love story and lovers are very serious. The piece should have the feel of an intimate moment between two people. He doesn't tell many people he's a loser superhero. Play it like the secret it is. When he speaks of the danger of being eaten it's because Isabella is a snacker, bananas, raspberries and corn chips they buy on Tuesday are gone by Wednesday. She's a little sensitive to her sensitivities. Try to make the piece more about her needs than about yours.

Scampi

Woman:

Could I . . . would you mind if I . . . I know this is going to be uncomfortable . . . you've made it clear I should never, well, come by your office. But, I'm here. I'm in your office which is, I don't know, a little more bare bones than I expected but . . . listen, last night when you took me out to dinner as, I want to get this right, "a thank you for being such a good friend" and I want to say I enjoyed the scampi . . . perfectly done and presented . . . good scampi. But just had to come and tell you how much . . . how extraordinarily much . . . that deeply and profoundly pissed me off, because if you ever took the time to notice, it would be clear to you, you bloody idiot, that I'm not just a "friend." I'm in love with you!! And a bunch of buttered shrimp doesn't deal with that! Sorry if all the other cubicles are listening but hey, slave labor, of Valiant Auto Insurance, listen up! I love William Cassidy and he's too stupid to notice! And if he has the common courtesy to drop by tonight when my roommate's at her AA meeting, I'm going to kiss his face off! Bye Bill, see you later, thanks for the overcooked scampi.

Performance Notes:

This piece thrives on misdirection. The character seems polite, even perhaps a little distant. If anything we should believe she has come to tell him she recognizes his interest in her but she's unavailable. Having misdirected us, boom, she reveals a totally different agenda and personality when she declares her love. It's almost like a split personality displayed. She isn't carefully putting him off, she's really infuriated that he can't see her interest in him. The next point is where in the text does she manage to control her outburst because you can't stay at that level forever? I think it's right after " . . . too stupid to notice." Pull down. Be as in control as possible and then lose it again on the last two words. " . . . overcooked scampi." A word about costuming. She wants him to think she looks great! Translate that into your own style sense. Also remember that at the beginning she tries to keep her voice down because of where she is and in the middle she doesn't care!

JUNIPERS

Man or Woman:

Wow. This is beautiful. The snow on the green of a thousand junipers. The wind. The cold is so sharp it's like cayenne pepper on your tongue. It's so seldom I feel anything. I don't mean watered down love or two-bit revenge, I mean a moment like this when you remember you have a body, and your body is in the world. I'm always so bundled up I don't even know what cold is. Sight, smell, hearing, taste, and touch. Really, I think I just pull myself together in the morning to get through the day, survive it but I don't touch the time, I don't smell it, I just cut through it like a ship's prow through water. The senses don't fill me up, Lou, and I think that leaves me empty when I get to you. What I need is for you to trace my face with the tip of your finger while the snow's falling, while there are all these junipers, because then I might feel something, and if that happened I might remember who you are.

Performance Notes:

Two people who are trying to salvage a relationship have gone to a State Park in the northwest in the dead of winter to ski and camp. What this character is seeing as she/he speaks is the pure, unadulterated beauty of the very beginning of the winter storm in the mountains. The speech is, in a way, a simple, heartfelt apology to someone you care about for the way you have allowed intimacy to slip away. The character is thinking hard as this speech goes on. Small pauses between some of the sentences or to choose a word or phrase will be helpful. After "I'm so sorry" the character finally turns and speaks directly to Lou. What is said then is gentle and direct without being sloppily sentimental. Use your senses during this speech —you need to see and smell and feel.

FLAT HATS

Woman:

I have this picture of me . . . well me and sixteen other little girls at dance class and we have these red and white checked blouses and blue tutus . . . little blue bow ties and little flat checked hats and tap shoes . . . remember how much you loved tap shoes? And we're all smiling and we have white gloves and our right hands are cocked over our heads like this and our left leg is bent at the knee. And I think we're thrilled. When I look at the picture I think we are. Miss Betty's Dance Studio. Wednesday afternoons, four to five thirty. And it just stabs me through the heart Rachel. I think what's wrong with me is I'm not part of a group. I don't get together with sixteen other anybodies doing anything in unison. I'm just with me, and maybe you, or maybe Truman, and it's lonely. Dance class is over and I'm in New York and I'm supposed to be enough for myself which is the big lie about growing up. Do we even know sixteen people who would get together with us for anything? Sixteen people who if we called them up would come over and do something in unison? God, life is sad.

Performance Notes:

The two people in the piece are probably sitting at a small table in a small downtown New York apartment. Maybe they've been for a walk, maybe they've been to the movies. This is your best and possibly only close friend in the city. She is talking about a photograph but it is not on the table. It's the memory of a photograph. You might start the piece sitting, then later get up and get a pot of coffee (mimed) and pour each of you refills. You might sit again for the final line. As to that final line, "God, life is sad," sad is not the tonality of the whole piece. If anything there is a more frustration than sadness present in the piece. The most important line is, "Do we even know sixteen people who would get together with us for anything?" that line should have focus and be a different moment then any other. "God life is sad" could even have a touch of bitter amusement or just be flat, practical truth. And she loves that photo.

Morrigan

Man or Woman:

So last summer my dad . . . my dad rode motorcycles . . . well, only one bike really, the Ducati Carbon, he thought everything else was bike-trash. He was a nice guy but this stuff, he was . . . unforgiving. My unforgiving dad. And he . . . uh . . . okay, he was screwed up . . . not real normal . . . he said Morrigan, some kind of Irish death god, had him at the top of the list. He could see Morrigan . . . he would point him out to me. He would be at the next table or some guy who went by in a convertible. So I'm going to guess Morrigan was riding double when he went off the mountain. And three days later I got a letter from him . . . from him and Morrigan, they both signed it. Well, maybe it wasn't a letter maybe it was a postcard and maybe it said "Having a wonderful time, wish you were here." That's the only thing I have from my dad. It's a good story, right? That's what my dad left me. . . a good story.

Performance Notes:

This audition piece is a scrap of conversation, and your job is to decide why and with whom. Let's say it's in reply to a long story (after a couple of drinks) in which the speaker's blind date has bored the bejabbers out of her with a long boring story about what he did last summer. Or, two soldiers trying to pass the time on a freezing night at a machine gun emplacement in Afghanistan. Or, two runners talking during a marathon. Situation is as important as content in this piece, and it's your decision. Make sure it's a situation that intrigues you. The second point is what the speaker feels about the father of whom he speaks? There are hints of dislike or a troubled childhood, of a situation in which a father's endless judgmental attitudes were hurtful and damaging to our character. There's bitterness here disguised as dinner conversation, make it real for yourself.

GREEN VEGETABLES

Woman:

You think this looks too girly? But you can't see where the tats were right? I tried a couple creams but that was bullshit so, hey, I had to do dermabrasion, which I don't care what they tell you, it sucks! I mean nobody likes being sanded, right? And one other thing, the numbing solution doesn't numb. You can still see the outline of the slacker's logo in the right light. Redlight, right? That was top SKA. But I moved on 'cause life is transformational or it fucking isn't life. So I'm into the girl-next-door shit which is where it's headed if you're on top of the curve. Some guy who wants a little wifey is going to get the surprise of his fucking suburban life, right? Things aren't what they appear. Keep that in mind, see. I think I'll learn to cook. I'm gonna cook little green vegetables. I'll hook up with some girl friends, meet a fuckin' lawyer in an uptown bar, do the romantic love retro thing. See what I think is, anybody you hook up with turns out to be a surprise. I want shoes with bows on them and a little silver necklace with a cross like you. See you out there.

Performance Notes:

Need something tough and uncompromising? Try this one. It takes place in the ladies' room at a speed dating competition. Our character is smoking and checking herself out in the mirror, perhaps applying lipstick, and chatting with a stranger who is next to her, who is probably appalled. After a checkered path and probably some really bad experiences with men she has decided that for financial reasons she needs to marry the kind of man she has never been interested in. At the end of the piece she checks out her repair work and heads off to fascinate some unsuspecting male. The tone here is cocky and amused. She can hardly imagine she would ever be doing this, but she is and she's surprised to find she's a little nervous. There's obviously a band and the "SKA" mentioned is probably SKA-punk which was a Jamaican precursor to reggae. So, cocky, a little loud, a little pissed-off at life and a little disdainful of the girl at the next mirror.

JOY

Man or Woman:

I-am-happy. Look at me, am I happy or what? I'm like bouncing around inside my shoes, Carla. Wilder than a sugar high and there's no down. I had a flat tire on the way to work today, it was like fun. Some guy stopped to help me and I said, "Hey sit and talk to me but I *like* changing this tire!" I dropped my iPhone in a diet coke and I laughed. I locked my keys in my car and all I could think was, "Damn I get to unlock this baby with a wire hanger!" Carla, you have to bring me down, I'm terrified. I'm like out of control. My body chemistry has locked on fast forward. What if that guy, whatshisname, the one whose face is pitted like the moon's craters, asks me out again? I'll probably say yes and I hate that guy. I feel like tap dancing and it is really, really creepy. I'm a depressive Carla, what's happened to me? You know what I was humming a minute ago? Zip-e-dee-do-dah! I'm like a cheerleader. Oh my God, I'm like a cheerleader! What if I stay this way? For God's sake Carla, do something, the smiles stuck. I can't stop. Help me. Help me. Help me!

Performance Notes:

A good choice for a relatively high energy actor and a dangerous choice for more reflective types. You do have to choose audition pieces that bear some resemblance to your personality. This is a character trapped in a mood much like a claustrophobic trapped in an elevator. It should feel a little bit like being possessed. So there's a manic stage here. And under that a trapped soul trying to get out. Is that something you can play? Take the line, "I feel like tap dancing and it is really, really creepy." Both feelings need to be present. The first half is way up and the second half horrified . . . and in one sentence! The key line in the piece is, I'm a depressive Carla, what happened to me? If, as I assume you will be, you've been playing a rapid pace, slow down this line and emphasize it. This is the line you want to have remembered. Remember also that at the end you have three, "help me's." Each should be different and the third separated by a pause from the other two.

WELCOME

Man or Woman:

You're the new guy, right? Welcome to the seventh circle of hell, new guy. You look nice, fresh, recently bathed, ready to go, upwardly mobile. You have no idea what you've got yourself into, do you? You see that machine over there? To your left. Yeah. Tri-Commutual weight loader. Piece of equipment costs maybe 600 million. We call it Lucifer 'cause it don't like us. No joke. It catches your sleeve, shirt tail, watch band, shoelace, it pulls you in and you come out manburger. We got seven pieces of machinery that can kill you. You lose your concentration, you bleed. You got a wedding ring on. Nice. The married guys leave little good-bye notes with the floor manager, y'know just in case. But hey, you got a job, right? I'm Bennie. You live 'til lunch you come sit at my table. I'll fill you in new guy, give you a few strategies. Keep you alive for the little lady. See you.

Performance Notes:

Whether played by man or woman this is a tough, bitter human exploited by the system. Probably the new guy is replacing someone seriously injured by the machine described. Probably there is no union protection here for the workers. Possibly the person speaking was once one of few workers trying to unionize this shop and failing, was demoted from a white collar job to this shop floor. It's hot in here, noisy and grimy. You are both physically uncomfortable. This is probably a late morning ten-minute work break. You noted the new guy earlier and nobody was talking to him. You walk up and offer your hand. There is an element of enjoying the process of scaring him with your information. If played by a woman there is a touch (not overdone) of flirtation. The tone is both cocky and depressed at the same time. This character has seen-it-all. There might be the physical business of cleaning oil off your hands or wiping the sweat away. When the piece ends with, "see you," the conversation is probably broken off because you see a floor-manager coming. Having this conversation at all could get you fired.

PEAKS

Woman:

I want to make love outside, and not here, not in Brooklyn. I want to be up high, you and me, 16,000 feet, something like that, on a ledge with like the Himalayas all around us, scary as hell but beautiful, and the air is thin and cold and we climb under piles of white furs and we make love like it meant something for once. And then we would be alright. We would be good forever. We wouldn't like . . . squabble like we do, pick at each other, snipe. We would have this beautiful thing like a pure gold secret inside us. Two people, they gotta have a bond based in the remarkable. Otherwise love is just another thing, right, easy come, easy go, disposable, wrapped in plastic, good for maybe three months. What have we got like that? Name it. See what I mean?

Performance Notes:

A couple right at the edge of breaking up are talking late at night after a drink or two. The apartment they are in is small, claustrophobic. The only windows look out on the wall of another building. He has just said, "listen, can we just stop arguing and make love? Please." She gets up and moves away, shaking her head. She is filled with a longing for something beautiful, not this. She doesn't look directly at him until the line, "and then we would be alright." She moves her chair closer to his and speaks gently, quietly. He doesn't respond and she moves away from him on the line, "two people, they gotta have a bond in the remarkable." The three months she speaks of is the duration of their relationship. The only real anger that escapes her is when she says, "name it?" there is a pause while she waits for his answer. He says nothing. Then she says the final line of the piece.

Four Ball

Man:

So, Benny and me we were shooting some four ball at this place on Creeson called Changwon Grill, where a bunch of Korean hustlers hang out. The Koreans they stick the cue ball beside the red ball for the opening shot. Who knows why. Anyways, we were a few bucks up and this old guy, and I mean old, walks up and throws a couple hundred dollar bills on the table, wants to play. I say to Benny, "Don't touch this guy, he's probably the ex red-ball champ of Korea or some crap." But Benny laughs me off and the old gentleman cleans his clock . . . wipes him out. Cleans the table three times running. Benny never takes a shot. Then he walks over and puts his finger on Benny's nose and says "don't come down here again" in real good English. And Benny, you know, like a reflex, knocks his hand away and eight guys come from no where, and stick nine millimeters in his face! The guys smile and we smile and we leave. So the lesson I take from this is everybody has a home court. Never mess with a hustler on his home court. Amen. Pass me a beer, my hands are still shaking.

Performance Notes:

This guy is really nervous, he's just experienced a very, very dangerous situation. He might even start by putting a hand out and seeing it is shaking. He might, during the opening lines take out a handkerchief and wipe his brow with it. He shakes his head after " . . . throws a couple of hundred dollar bills on the table, wants to play." He might get up from a chair, sit down again immediately and then get up again moments later. The loudest part of the audition is "eight guys have, come from nowhere, and stick nine millimeters in his face!" There's a significant pause after . . . "and we leave." He's really thinking it over. The "amen" is truly heartfelt and he really needs that beer. The point here is to make it the aftermath of an experience that scared him out of his wits. If you can play that and make us believe it the piece will work extremely well for you.

HOLD ME, TOUCH ME

Woman:

All right, all right, please, you're my sister so, so is this love? Because I'm not the type, right? You're like the beautiful, soulful one and I'm acknowledged to be the jock. The one who has guy friends, and yatta, yatta, yatta. I mean, I'm a disaster with love, right? Last time I force the guy to go camping, he gets bit by a coral snake and I have to take him to emergency. Now he won't talk to me. But, but this guy in my head. I have these constant whattayacallums, fantasies, but not sexy, not hold me-touch me's. I'm just playing soccer with the guy, that's my fantasy. I kind of follow him around, for what I don't know. So you're my sister, what's going on here? Yesterday, he's talking to a guy and I think, I should go over there and just throw him on the ground. I almost did that, Laura. But then what? What would I do with him when he's on the ground? I have no instincts for this but somehow, some way, I don't want to screw it up. Put down the eye-liner, give me guy advice or I'm going to whack you. I'm not kidding here, advise me! Advise me, or else!

Performance Notes:

This woman is not used to emotions overwhelming her and not only doesn't understand it, she definitely doesn't like it. I think she hasn't been close to this "sister," who is an entirely different type, for some time but has suddenly shown up. The sister is surprised by the visit but is getting ready to go out with her fiancé. She's putting on her makeup and not giving full attention, which makes you crazy. Maybe the imaginary sister is sitting in a chair and you work the piece around her. You're confused and that makes you edgy, even angry. She doesn't have "fantasies" and she doesn't like them. She is half begging, half demanding on " . . . what's going on here." I would spread the line so there is a slight pause after each word. She is truly confused on, "what would I do with him when he's on the ground?' This is a practical person confronted with what she considers impractical thoughts. She feels like she's been taken over by an alien. "Advise me, or else" is an actual threat.

DRY MOUTH

Woman:

I have to get off the dextroamphetamines. The time has come, seriously. I got dry mouth, I got increased heart rate, I got euphoria, I got constipation. Somebody asked me did I have Tourette's? You want me to walk around, and have people think I have Tourette's? Is that who you want me to be? I'm getting tics on top of my tics. Facial stuff that is get-

175

ting attention paid to me that I'm not looking for in the least. I'm at the point where I want to be . . . need to be nothing at all, anonymous. I want to go to parties with you and when I look around no one is looking at me. I want to be the chick in the corner. I want to be absent, translucent, invisible because then maybe I could heal and be good for you instead of what I am, because you know and I know this isn't working out and I need this. I need you. Right, go on, walk away, and get me to understand I'm disposable. You called me beautiful? Where's that time? You got me into this, you dealt me in, now tell me how the hell to get out? Go screw yourself. Right, slam the door.

Performance Notes:

This is an angry woman at the end of her rope. Her boyfriend is probably a dealer. This conversation has probably been going on for some time. There is a build in intensity throughout the piece. The first sentences could even be her talking to herself until the line, "you want me to walk around and have people think I have Tourette's?" at that point she moves closer to him and the intensity grows but it is nowhere near shouting. On, " . . . then maybe I could be good for you . . ." the tone softens, a memory of how she used to love him. From, "right, go on, walk away . . ." the intensity grows to a shout on " . . . now tell me how to get out?" "Go screw yourself", drops down into cold rationality. "Right. Slam the door." is again to herself almost whispered. She might have a physical "tic", as she mentions but be careful not to overuse it. Three or four times is enough. The piece can be done standing or sitting. If this is the only piece you are doing you shouldn't use a chair. If it is paired with something more physical then sitting is fine. She's strung out. She itches. She hasn't slept, her eyes smart. Examine the piece's physical side.

GABRIEL

Woman:

I see angels all the time, they're all around me with diaphanous wings and scarlet robes. Pure spirits, messengers. Cherubim and seraphim, and sometimes they take bodily shape like you. Because your name is Gabriel, you told me that in the bookstore. Gabriel was sent twice to the prophet Daniel and now you've been sent to me. You want a taco, I can't eat all this? You think I'm nuts, right? But I see you, I hear you, when you come in or go out there's a thrumming like hummingbirds. I get it. "Be not forgetful to entertain strangers, for thereby some have entertained angels unaware." You want another cup of coffee? I'll get you whatever you want because I want your guidance. I need your guidance because I lack direction, but that's over now because you're here. When angels kiss you it's like a brand, it burns and purifies and I want your kiss. I have to go back to work Gabriel but I'll be at early Mass at St. Anthony's. Come to me there, unfurl your eagles wings and give me purpose. Gabriel, listen to me, you leave the tip, okay? I don't have change. "Bring from above, echoes of mercy, whispers of love." See you at Mass.

Performance Notes:

This character has problems in her life. Perhaps a bad relationship, perhaps money problems, maybe she cares for an ill parent. Gabriel's presence however has calmed her. Whether he is actually an angel or not is beside the point . . . she "knows" he is. As she says, she sees angels all the time but this is the first time one has taken human shape. She has just finished eating with Gabriel in a fast food joint over lunch. She stands up and begins searching in her bag for tip money, which she never finds. She might also put on a coat or jacket, which is placed over the back of the chair. She speaks to Gabriel in a straightforward almost intimate way. We should not think this character is crazy but there is some fierce joy in her eyes. Gabriel is the solution to her problems. There is one strong, almost angry moment when she says, "I need your guidance because I need direction . . ." she knows she has been too loud and that people are staring at her. She is attracted to him and the line about wanting to kiss is momentarily filled with need and longing. The next moment that disappears and is replaced by a matter-of-fact tonality. The final line, "see you at Mass" is spoken as she walks away.

FLAT SCREEN

Woman:

See, can't live in one place. I can't see the same walls. This sofa? I can't look at it. I can't sit on it. This place is over for me. I get vertigo from being in this room. I get ill from walking in here and seeing you in the chair in front of the flat screen. You're okay. You're one okay, guy. But you have too many limits, Josie. There's too many words you don't say. Too many thoughts you don't think. To many jokes you don't get. I should be satisfied, I know that. I was with a guy who hit me, you would never do that. My brother always said I was going to screw myself up with too many expectations. And that has come true like a bullet in my brain. I have to be around a guy like firelight, you know? Something has to change every few minutes, and who can do that? Anyway, I'm going. Cars all packed. I think I'll go south, Josie. It doesn't really matter you know, just so the movie rolls. You'd be a good thing for a normal person. Don't get down on yourself. Got to go.

Performance Notes:

In a way this is my favorite type of audition piece. One grounded in relationship. We've all cared for someone we wished was a little smarter, a little more able to help us understand the life we're living and leaving such a person is hard because they probably have other virtues and qualities. The woman in this piece, has to care for Josie, she has to wish she didn't have to leave him and she knows it isn't fair. There is deep regret in her line, " I should be satisfied, I know that." She in fact knows, in a bone deep way what she has " . . . too many expectations. By the time she gets to, "anyway, I'm going." The tone has to change significantly. It needs to harden and lose its empathy. She feels pulled to stay and she does not want to, in fact, cannot. Her empathy returns in full force once more for, "you'd be a good thing for a normal person." But then there is something mechanical and final in "got to go." The angriest moment (and there shouldn't be too many) comes earlier on with, "I get ill from walking in here and seeing you in that chair in front of that flat screen." This is a piece about having to harden your heart to save yourself.

VICTIMS

Man:

Damn! Spring and all that shit. Gives me hope and expectations and general all around optimism. You probably think that's weird for a serial killer, right? Hey, we got the same biology, we got the same response to a crow in the snow or a crape myrtle pink against the purple of the horizon. I mean it wakes up my heart, buddy. Puts a smile on my face. Get's me to thinking about the pure joy of walking down a street where there's a bunch of saucer magnolias and picking me out a victim! I mean in the winter!, I'm shoveling snow, splitting wood, patching up the gutters, I just turn in on myself like an old bear. I'm just sustaining life, just trying to get on through, keep warm, pop me some popcorn, just don't have the time, energy or instinct to take a life. But hey, the forsythia is lemon yellow against the steady green of the junipers and I am ready to go! Honey, there's no use straining yourself against those ropes. You're just going to bruise your pure ivory skin and I DON'T LIKE THAT!

Performance Notes:

Here's a killer with a romantic and sentimental response to spring and flowers in the snow! The fun part of doing this speech is that it has an ordinary, even pleasant tone until the last line. You don't have to work at having a danger-ous subtext or chilling oddity. Just be the pleasant self you ordinarily are and then turn loose the danger and violence in the last line. It's a 'surprise' piece and the surprise is the violence in the last three words. Don't ruin it by letting us see that in you earlier—go to an imaginary window around "gets one to thinking about the pure joy of walking down a street . . ." Finally he turns and looks at the victim trussed up, on the flow and kneels by her on "honey, there's no use straining yourself against these ropes." He rises once more just before the final line. Remember to allow yourself your natural charm until the piece turns.

BUTTER

Woman:

End of the line and we are really, really there, aren't we? Just popped out like a Jack-in-the-box when we least expected it. Oh well, it's only love, right? As far as I can tell everybody gets second, third, fifteenth chances. My sister says every-body marries the fifth person you fall in love with and sadly, you're only number three. So, listen, just so I can get better for number four, I could use some tips on my most obvious mistakes. I know I talk too much. I've never fallen in love but what that came up . . . but you don't talk and I don't like the radio on so I'm really just entertaining myself and I don't like silence when there's somebody with a perfectly functional mouth sitting there staring at me! Sorry, didn't mean to yell. What else? Sleeping in t-shirts, I know you hate that. The fact that I'm smarter than you are, let's just call that breaks of the game. The fact that people like me and they don't like you, that's a biggie. You know what? I don't really care that you're leaving now that I think about it. If I didn't have unforgivable faults I'd be stuck with you. And by the way, I eat butter out of the container with my fingers before I put it on the table! I go through your wallet when you're sleeping and I hide the condoms so we can't have sex. Bye now.

Performance Notes:

This is a cheerful piece about getting away from a person you don't want to be with for another thirty seconds. You might be sipping from a thirty-two ounce cola or nibbling on a chocolate bar. She's wearing a little spring dress in an adorable color and there's something about her that reminds us of a *cute*, bouncy thirteen-year-old even though she's twenty. She gets distracted during the piece and checks out her newly done finger nails and possibly re-does her makeup. This was definitely a cheerleader in high school and perhaps someone studying musical theatre in college. She's charming, even delightful until she yells "and I don't like silence when there's somebody with a perfectly functional mouth sitting there staring at me!" immediately after this outburst she's back to her positive self. Hopefully the piece is funny as well as dramatic and it's always a benefit when an audition piece serves both those masters.

LOOKING

Man:

No, I really like looking at you. You're really elegant in space. You wear the yellow dress and you lean against the garden wall just off-center with your head slightly cocked and your arms behind you. It tears my heart out! And you sit . . . I mean you are a genius at sitting. I counted one night you sat nine different ways in a half hour. I mean you really worked that chair and every way you sat there turned me on. I mean talking is completely overrated in relationships, we use up whatever good stuff we've got and then it's just noise, but looking! People who make a good look wherever they are, people who compliment architecture, and go color on color? Those people are lifetime sexy. How could you ever get tired of them? How could I ever get tired of you? Listen, I wonder if you would stand at the picture window with that blue-gray sweater against the background of the forsythias and spread your arms all the way out like you did last Wednesday. Because then I would have to propose to you, there wouldn't be any choice. Oh my God, that looks wonderful.

Performance Notes:

This is obviously a love story based on one of the senses, seeing. Seeing this woman is like a series of pleasurable explosions in this man's head. How can he explain that? And that "how" is the acting secret of this piece. She doesn't feel what she sees in the same way. He is trying to find words to explain visual pleasure to a non-visual person. He struggles. He fights to find just the right word. He feels that it's crucial she understands but fears it's like trying to pledge your love to a person who doesn't speak English. He says a couple of sentences and then stops dead because he fears she can't understand. He starts again trying to make gestures that clarify his thoughts. He tries, he fails, he tries again. Finally he realizes that what he's doing is proposing marriage. She smiles finally and holds her arms out as requested. His final line, "oh my God that looks wonderful" is a moment of triumph. He gets what he wants . . . her!

THE BARD

Woman:

I used to wear these red bell bottoms and a white tank top . . . real retro-look and it attracted criminals. Really. If I'd had a place to put them, I could have cleaned up Philadelphia. It had a particular impact on forgers. I mean you don't meet many forgers but wearing that outfit I met two in a row. This one guy forged art. He specialized in Andy Warhol, you know, baking soda boxes and stuff like that. I had a car-jacker, a crooked accountant and a guy who had killed his mother. I couldn't figure it out until I made the connection to my wardrobe. So, as a test, I put on the ensemble and took my Brittany Spaniel for a walk and this guy hit on me, you know, using the dog as an excuse and you know who he turned out to be? Bernie Madoff's son. Bingo. So to protect and diversify my love life I had to get rid of the outfit. I gave it to my sister and she's engaged to a guy who does home invasion. He's nice. So to quote the bard, "there are more things in heaven and earth Horatio, than are dreamt of in your philosophy." Life's a mystery, celebrate it.

Performance Notes:

This woman's life is a constant surprise to her. She shakes her head in amazement at the things that happen. She knows the person she's talking to will have a hard time believing her story. The key is, she wants to be believed. She's emphatic. She's talking to an old friend who she knows is a practical person. How do you get such a person to believe such an eccentric experience? She tries to talk in a simple, rational way. Her underlying message is, of course, the last line "Life's a mystery, celebrate it." It may be that the person she is talking to may have just broken up with someone because they had a criminal record. And her answer is, basically, "give the guy a chance!" leave yourself open. This is an optimistic person who's message is: wade in, get your hands dirty. Find reason to *do* things not reasons *not to*. Maybe you should eat a banana while you do the piece. Or maybe she's exercising. This is a multitasker. A New Jersey accent would be cool. She plays the last line like a newspaper headline or a giant print ad on a skyscraper. Make us feel her energetic optimism!

B<small>AD</small> B<small>LOOD</small>

Man or Woman:

You can say what you want to me, Mama. You can call me lazy, like you do, and deceitful, hapless and hopeless and a tattooed disgrace to the family and it's just like water off a ducks back! Hell, I know I'm bad, that was clear as a bell when I shaved Sissies' head while she was sleeping back in third grade. I've killed dogs and cats and other domestic style animals. I've set fires and blown up abandoned vehicles. Hell, I filled up the mayor's son's car with wet cement and peed in the product when I worked in the pie factory. You think I'm not aware of my nature? Mama you got to make do with the cards you got dealt. You can't shirk it, you gotta work it! So, I'm taking off on Monday, gonna rob Taco Bells coast to coast and then I'm coming back here to Bathsheba, Texas and buy you the kind of duplex you deserve and that Juki DDL-8700 high-speed single needle lock stitch industrial sewing machine you've been wanting all your life. I may be the devil, Mama, but I'm your little devil and I will make you proud of my black, burned heart. Hug me Mama, I'm gonna bring it all home for you.

Performance Notes:

This is the moment when you finally tell a parent who you really are and not who they wish you are. The character starts out pacing back and forth almost like a caged lion. She/he stops stock still on "Hell, I know I'm bad . . ." She/he sits down on "you think I'm not aware of my nature?" she/he has been trying to decide whether to leave or stay so "so I'm taking off on Monday" is a decision. She/he has cased Taco Bells, she has worked in Taco Bells, she *knows* how to rob Taco Bells and she's on her way! She probably has no-good brothers who do little or nothing to help their mother. She loves her mama and is excited to do something for her, and she knows exactly what her mama wants, and she's *proud* to know it! She gets more and more excited about what she's going to do. There 's a physical excitement. If she knew how to do a backflip, she'd do it. If she sits in a chair she sits with it back to front, astride it. The build in her excitement 'til it reaches a crescendo is crucial. Let it all out!

CLASSICAL PIECE

Man or Woman:

I hate Shakespeare. First of all, the dude didn't write his own plays. Secondly, there's no reason he couldn't write plain English because he is a native born English speaker, and, thirdly, I got to do that pretentious shit just to get into some Godforsaken college theatre department and thus insure I will never make a living as an adult? Just, hey, let me put the economics to one side. Get this, "But let the ruffian Boras once enrage the gentle Thetis and anon behold our bark bounding between the two moist elements like Perseus' horse, where's sides but even now co-rivalled greatness?" the hell is that about? I am not paying $35,000 dollars in tuition, plus nine thousand for housing and six thousand for French fries to say that shit. If they don't say it on *CSI-Miami,* I'm not saying it. You want a classical piece, I'll do something from the damn *Godfather*. Shakespeare has had his fifteen minutes of fame, okay? If I have to study a foreign language, I'll take Arabic alright, because I can do something with that. "Perseus' horse," my ass.

Performance Notes:
Warning: Don't do this piece for Shakespeare festivals!

The character isn't angry, he/she is in their own mind, simply logical. The situation is that the character is doing an audition for *Much Ado About Nothing* and stops in the middle, steps forward and speaks. He has, in his life, auditioned for six Shakespeare's and never gotten a part. When he does, "First, second and third" he ticks them off on his fingers like a grocery list. He does get seriously ticked off when he talks about the money he's spending for college, after all he is the consumer! When he does the Shakespeare quote he does it without emphasis in a more or less robotic cadence. He's been told he isn't a stage actor but a television or film actor and that's where his entire focus is. Probably he starts standing downstage of a chair, probably sitting after, "if they don't say it on CSI-Miami, I'm not saying it!" after ". . . because I can do something with that." He rises and says the last line as he walks off-stage. You stop, of course, before you disappear. It is, lest we forget, an audition.

RATMAN

Woman:

You ever listen to your body, Ratman? All the sounds, functions hissing and bumbling in there while you try and fall asleep? You ever think what your body does with all those macadamia nuts you put in there? See, the body is the assembly line, and you are the product that gets delivered to market. What kinda product you putting out, Ratman? I got to say if you are the product they got real bad quality control down in your factory, man. Your endocrine system, your digestive system, your cardiovascular system doing all that good work to produce a second rate pimp? Just how is it possible your insides could evolve into a system so beautiful and functional and your outside is about to get itself arrested because of it's Cro-Magnon, witless activities, because I have called the police. Yeah me, I did that. Your thing, your cow, your meal ticket, your "mini boppa" got up off her knees and cut your nuts. Go ahead, hit me face-on on the way out, Ratman, it's way worth the blood, it's cool.

Performance Notes:

A woman at the moment she gets rid of her pimp. It would

be wonderful if she was putting on eye makeup and lipstick while she did this. She has a strangely off-hand manner in the first half, as if it were an ordinary day at the office. She probably finishes what ever makeup work she is doing after, ". . . second rate pimp." She then turns and talks directly to the gentleman. You should spread out the line " . . . I-have-called-the-police" with a slight pause between each word. After that she builds in volume and anger until underplaying the last two words, "it's cool." She probably finishes with a ravishing smile. She's free. I should note that this piece does not need to be played "tough" or "lower class." Be yourself in the situation and it will work for you.

THE DOWN PAYMENT

Woman:

So, what I'm going to do now, Artie . . . and I hope you agree, although that's not altogether necessary. I am going to take the number 1 bus to your dad's house and I'm going to tell him we are getting married although you haven't formally asked me yet and I am going to make it clear to him that I am not, as you just told me he told you, a slut. But rather, I am the backbone you are so sorely missing and that I will organize you and give you a purpose and, if necessary choose a profession for you, in which I will see that you excel. And you will be happy Artie, happy to be dominated and glad to accept the secondary role in our home in which you will be calm and supportive and make me happy. Now I know you have an engagement ring you have been planning to give me because I go through your clothes when you're asleep. Give it to me because I want to be wearing it when I see your father and explain to him I am not a slut and he needs to lend us forty thousand dollars for a down payment on the house I found. Thank you. Now sit down and watch some sports or something and when I get back our life will begin. Love you sweetie. Bye.

Performance Notes:

She is warm, pleasant and smiling. Because she is, and has been for some time, in charge of the relationship, she doesn't have to bulldoze him. What we see is the logical end of her long term dominance. After she has seen he posesses an engagement ring but isn't giving it to her, she realizes she must fully take the controls. She is very firm when she said "give it to me because I want to be wearing it when I see your father . . ." She puts out her hand, palm up, to receive it and puts it on her finger during the next sentence, admiring it in the light. She gives him a kiss on the cheek after saying, "thank you." For the rest of the speech she treats him rather like a third grader, waving to him on the way out. What's necessary here is that she displays some real charm so that we understand his being involved with her. It's key that she play that she knows he'll like the life with her. And he probably will.

HEARTS

Woman:

I finally figured out the guy was blind. Stone blind and he had practiced every detail of this date we were on over and over and over. Probably a hundred times. Knew the menu. Had eaten the tilapia over spinach in practice sessions. Could walk to the men's room exactly like a sighted person. Is that not touching? Is that not a will of steel? And he had accomplices in the restaurant so when he came back from the restroom he could compliment me, in detail, on my dress and jewelry. It doesn't matter how I figured it out, that's immaterial. It doesn't matter why, for God's sake, he didn't want me to know. What matters is how much he wanted me to like him before he told me. I mean I've been on dates where the guy doesn't even bother to wear a clean shirt and he knew the exact number of steps from my apartment to the restaurant! You know how I've been saying I didn't just want a relationship I wanted a romance? Bingo. He told me after he kissed me. And you know what I said? "when can I see you again?" and he smiled a smile so big, so happy, so real it enlarged my heart. So, that's what I did tonight, what about you?

Performance Notes:

This is a young woman who didn't feel she was a romantic, finding romance. She's talking to her sister who waited up to see how the date went. The speaker is in the midst of an adrenaline rush. She wasn't expecting much out of the date, she hardly knew him. Maybe they met in a grocery store. And it had blown her mind. Maybe this comes on the heels of the end of a long term relationship and she is highly defended against men in general. In any case, when the piece starts she's excited and amazed. The amount of work he put into the evening with her! She finally calms herself down around " . . . I mean I've been on dates. . ." The last part of the speech is a confession of feelings she didn't expect, to someone who didn't expect her to feel them. She slows down, choosing her words carefully. She sees just before the last sentence that her sister is dumbfounded by her story and in the last moment, teases her.

BLUE MOON

Man or Woman:

I never liked sunsets and I hate the night. I get anxious when it gets dark, I get this foreboding. It makes me thinking about death and how I'll die and what being nothing is. What it means for this to be over and what exactly and precisely I've done with the time I was given and worse, what I didn't do? So that's why I was so quiet when you asked me if the moon wasn't incredibly beautiful. Because the moon is dead, it's dust, it's a reminder of what's to come. Do you have a cigarette? Hard to love a depressive, huh? I'm really sorry, but it has an upside, I can tap dance. The secret of life is that black moods can't survive tap. Watch this. And this. Now here comes the big finish. Anyway I love you too. You've noticed I'm good during the day, just stay away from me at night. We can get married, have two apartments, I'll be with you 'til 7 p.m. and we can have breakfast at dawn. That's what I'm afraid of. Can we go back inside? I don't like it out here.

Performance Notes:

Okay, to do this piece you have to be able to tap dance. Anybody reading further? It does allow actor/dancers a chance to audition both skills. So, this piece needs a jacket because it's an October night and a little chilly. It's a quiet piece that would make a good companion to something more vocally aggressive. While the speaker claims to be depressive, he/she is not depressed. Remember this is a marriage proposal, albeit a very specific one. The person being spoken to has just declared his/her love for the speaker. These two have been a couple for a good while and both of them know it's time for the next step . . . either marriage or they need to go their own ways. The speaker, we need to remember, has a gentle sense of humor about depression and that needs to be an acting component here. And the tap should be . . . well . . . pretty good. The speaker is semi-serious about the odd way he/she suggests conducting the marriage. Notice the listener doesn't immediately agree. There should be a solid pause after "half a life is better than none, right?" the speaker is afraid he/she is being turned down. But that we don't know for sure.

MUSIC OF THE SPHERES

Man or Woman:

I'm here because I can hear my organs working. I mean hear, okay, like you hear a garbage truck going by? Doctor, my entire body is like a construction site . . . or a community orchestra in South Dakota. I can hear deoxygenated blood being pumped from my heart to my lungs and I'm a theatre major. How am I supposed to do Chekhov when I'm distracted by my pancreas breaking down my stomach contents? What's really irritating, and I mean nutsoid, is when my kidneys filter metabolic waste! It's like an instrumental version of Lady Gaga doing Paper Gangsta! Help me. I don't have a life, I have a cacophony. I end up doing things in rhythm with my bladder gurgling. I don't even want to go into what it does to making out with my girlfriend/boyfriend. And don't tell me to call a therapist, I'd rather go to a contractor and get sound proofing. Oh-oh. Oh-oh. it's starting up. Its my endocrine system doing the downbeat . . . can you hear my thyroid and my adrenals? Whoa baby, here comes the urethra! Gotta dance, doctor. Gotta rock my digestive system. Back off, I gotta dance!

Performance Notes:

Think about it. What if you continually heard your organs doing their work. Yes, it would drive you mad as a hatter! However we need to play this piece more as a comic irritation than as a tragedy. The speaker is anatomically knowledgeable. She knows where the organs are located and points to those areas as they come up. There's a little bit of gothic-humor in here too. It's like Dracula is coming when he/she says, "oh-oh. oh-oh. it's starting up." Now this is a comic physical piece as well, his body does start to dance at the end of the piece in a weird, jerky fashion. If you have a dancer friend get them to choreograph it for you. When the dialogue finishes the organ-dance goes on for another five seconds and then the performer finds stillness and the piece is over. Oh, at the beginning the speaker is working against the fact that she's not sure if she will be believed by the doctor. It's a good obstacle to overcome, use it.

JAM

Man:

Get out of the car, man. Because I want your car. I'm taking your car. It's not gonna be your car, it's gonna be my car. I'm gonna sell this baby for parts and then I'm gonna buy thousand dollar sneakers. Nine pair. Okay, okay, you are not paying attention and to not pay attention is to irritate me, and to irritate me is to get shot. See this? This is a Walther PPQ, a short recoil operated, lock-breach weapon with the barrel engaging the slide with the single large lug entering the ejection window. Whattaya mean what do I mean? I mean get out of the car! Get out of the car, get out of the car, get out of the car! This is freaking nuts!! The light is green, we are holding up traffic, horns are blowing, gimme your car! All right, all right, gimmie your wallet and we'll call it even. Great, there's a cop over there. Fine. Twenty bucks. I would murder you, but I can't murder you in a traffic jam with a cop walking over here. Okay, five bucks. This is insane! Fine, forget it, have a nice day.

Performance Notes:

This piece has a very clear arc from being cocky and in charge at the beginning to being panicky and out of control at the end. A good arc often makes for a very good audition. You don't need a prop, a finger-thumb gun will work just fine. After being totally confident the situation begins to fray with the line "okay, okay, you are not paying attention . . ." you get a little more hyper. The next step up in the speakers panic and disintegration comes with "get out of the car, get out of the car, get out of the car!" why isn't the driver doing what he says?! Now there is a physicality of looking around frantically at the traffic piling up. The final straw is when you see the cop. Now you actually beg and finally, as the cop starts walking over, you panic and run. Be absolutely sure what you play at the beginning of the piece isn't what you play at the end. It's crucial.

DAD

Man or Woman:

So this . . . this isn't very complicated, sis. It's as bad as brain surgery but it isn't brain surgery. We just need to drink several beers and decide whether we should read Dad's diaries. Can you believe this? 1963 through 2011 in individual black, lined diaries with big green rubber bands around them. What's in them? And why do we want to know? Do we want to know? I'm sorry, why couldn't the guy just die and be gone? I mean, I loved him, I did, but what's with this? He was . . . you could set your clock by his habits. He was an accountant. What does an accountant have to write in 48 diaries? And come to think of it, why did he always take his vacations by himself? And why did clients call in the middle of the night? And who were half those people at the funeral? And the guy who fired his pistol in the air in the graveyard and then split? I don't know. I think I like the dad I knew. I think that's the dad I want to keep. Burn 'em.

Performance Notes:

A very human situation. How much do we actually want to know about our parents? And I mean really! The key line (and it needs to be played differently than any other moment in the piece) is "and, hey, do we want to know?" you have be extremely conflicted and worried. The funeral was obviously a wild and mysterious affair and needs to be played as such. This piece probably takes place at night after the funeral so it is completely fresh in their minds. The piece starts sitting down but you should get up and pace starting with " . . . why did he always take his vacations by himself?" You then stop stock still on "and who was that guy who fired his pistol in the graveyard and then split?" Then finally sit back down for the final two words, "Burn 'em." This is a piece where we really need to see you think. It's like a nervous detective trying to put clues together. It also moves from, "I can't decide" to deciding. Get that in there.

THE VISITOR

Man or Woman:

Who are you? You're sitting in my apartment. You're eating food from my refrigerator . . . how the hell did you get in here? In case your interested, you're scaring the hell out of me but I'm a little calmed down by the fact you're wearing a really expensive suit. Do I know you? Are you a friend of Dad's? okay, I'm calling 911. Hello? A guy has broken into my apartment . . . some guy, I don't know. Yeah he's still here. 58 Southside, ground floor apartment. Yeah. Yeah. Thanks. On their way, five minutes. Whoa! A gun. Okay. I don't like this. The gun thing . . . I don't like the gun thing . . . Holy crap! Look . . . Look, don't shoot yourself, don't . . . listen I don't know who you are, why you're here, what the deal is, but I'm asking you not to shoot yourself. You want to talk about it? Tell me why? Please, talk to me, there's always a way out, it's never so bad . . . look I'm a kid, this is way, way outside my pay grade . . . life is precious, I know that much . . . you can't take it and get it back so don't . . . Noooo! Oh, Man! He's all over me. He's all over my clothes. What the hell were you doing in my apartment?!!

Performance Notes:

A realistic horror tale. A guy you don't know breaks into your apartment and kills himself. In the first moment there's surprise and fear but to do this piece you have to fully picture what the intruder is doing and how on a moment to moment basis you interpret the intruder's intent. He doesn't seem hostile or dangerous. He's sitting at a table eating leftovers from your fridge. His manner is neutral. He doesn't seem threatening. He does not react to your questions. He watches you and eats. You don't seem to trouble him. After a bit he lifts a gun from his lap. Now your alarm system goes into overdrive. Your tone is different, your physicality is different. This is real, genuine danger! Suddenly he puts the barrel of the gun into his mouth. Once more our mood catapults into a different place. Suddenly from being the hunted you become the negotiator, even his savior. You try to be calm rational empathetic, he shoots himself. Now you are horrified and disbelieving. That's the trip, from startled and afraid, to personal panic, to trying to stop a suicide, to horrified. An excellent acting trip in ninety-seconds.

BYE

Man or Woman:

You broke it. Out of all my stuff you . . . was this . . . was this on purpose or . . . I told you . . . right you remember this? That was from Mom you idiot. What else do I have from her? I'm sorry, I can't believe this! There is my stuff and your stuff and I told you, stay away from my stuff. As long as you are here, as long as I am putting you up, letting you crash, letting you waste your life as usual, try to leave my life intact, if that's not too much to ask? I mean really, you are like bad karma personified, Hunter. And I'm sorry, I feel for you, I do, but I have told you for years that I'm not going down with you. I'm not an extension of your screwed-up-ness. You're smiling, right? You think this is funny because in your life it doesn't matter what breaks because you don't care. You are past caring Hunter, but hey, I am not. I'm not! So I'm sorry and I know . . . I know in the scheme of things this was just an accident, a blink. But things start somewhere and they end somewhere and this is it. This is where it ends. Pack up.

Performance Notes:

The actor starts staring at the floor. Shortly the actor kneels down and picks up an imagined shard of broken porcelain and a couple of lines later tosses it away. After " . . . if that's not too much to ask?" He/she turns to leave the room and then turns back for "I mean really . . ." there's a pause before, "you're smiling, right?" After "I'm not." the character makes the final decision that Hunter *must* leave. There's a final pause before "pack up." These are, I know, blocking details mainly, but important. The piece itself concerns how a small event, an even not-in-itself terribly important moment provokes an emotion that leads to a larger decision. The acting takes hold and I think it most powerfully happens on, "you are past caring, Hunter, but hey, I am not. I'm not!" let that emotion out for that one line and that line only. Contain the rest of the time.

STUFF

Man or Woman:

How many objects are in here, Momma? I don't know, who knows, maybe a quarter million? How many yard sales is this? How many salt and pepper shakers like pigs and presidents? And when you're gone, Mama, and we all go, right, where does all this go and who takes it there, in what series of rent-a-trucks, and how many days, weeks, hundreds of hours will this subtract from my life? You remember my life, Mama? Because I think you've always been like confused about the idea that there are two lives here, that it's not just one . . . yours. So, I love you, but please listen to me, you have got to stop buying figurines, and memory plates and yarn quilts, candlesticks, ashtrays, coffee mugs, Fiestaware, beer steins, decorative plug covers, toy tea sets and this whole tsunami of . . . this whole blizzard of, I'm sorry, brightly colored crap. Please, I beg of you, really I beg, 'cause you're enough. It's you I love but you're buried under this avalanche of not-you-ness. I want you, Momma, one mother not the mother of all objects. You have to stop, Momma, before I forget who you are.

Performance Notes:

This is something that our speaker has been suffering in silence about for many years. Maybe the piece is provoked by the mother returned from a yard sale with several bags of . . . well . . . junk. The piece can start high vocally, almost a shout, and then pulls down into a strained quiet on the line "how many salt and pepper shakers like pigs and presidents." He/she loses control again on . . . there are two lives here, that it's not just one . . . yours." And immediately pulls down again. It's a piece full of losing control and then achieving it again. When he/she lists the objects in the room you can turn in circles like a top, pointing at this and that. Finally you can actually kneel down on "Please, I beg of you, really I beg." You would rise in time to do the final line standing.

PARTY

Man:

All right, who drank the canola oil? You think I'm joking? The bottle is like leaking so I poured it into the empty wine bottle we use for watering the plants and when we were playing poker last night, somebody drank the canola oil. All the canola oil, 48 fluid ounces. And while you guys are not, you know, connoisseurs, it's possible you might know the difference between canola and Chablis. I'm not getting a lot of response here. My point is, what the hell, gentlemen, are we doing in college? We have the brains of migratory toads. We major in five card stud, alcoholic content and the elusive sexual encounter, at forty thousand a year on our parents nickel. We are not students, gentlemen, we are scoundrels. We are exactly what the society at large wishes not to produce. We are, in fact, so dim, so uncomprehending, so without the ability to make crucial distinctions that we drink canola oil! So before we cause overpopulation, global warming, the end of fossil fuels and a universal canola shortage I suggest we leave the campus and live in the woods like bears. Now who the hell was it who left their mother passed out on my bed?

Performance Notes:

This is an apartment with four male roommates. It is the morning after a party, and the speaker has had more than enough bacchanalia. Alone among the four he is probably paying for his own education. The canola oil is the straw that breaks the camel's back. His tone is that of cynical amazement. He seems friendly, even chummy, suppressing his anger, perhaps he is drying his hands on a dish towel or handkerchief. The only anger we can detect is on the final sentence. Another possible physicality is picking up imaginary party debris and putting it in an imaginary garbage bag. Take a healthy pause after " . . . know, the difference between canola and chablis." This is a big transitional moment. His mainly cool composure and sardonic delivery obviously masks his anger. That man is crucial to the piece. He is calm and collected (if amazed) as he confronts chaos.

ESSAY

Woman:

Let's just clarify what we're talking about, okay? No, stop, it's my turn to talk. My turn. Shut up, Jason! Fact one, I let you look at the paper I wrote on Egyptian Tomb Furniture at the college I transferred in from. Fact two, you kept it for a week. Fact three, you ripped if off for your art history class. Whole paragraphs word for word, Jason. Don't screw with me. Fact four, you win the Terra Augustine Essay prize, you get it published and pocket one thousand dollars and then you drop by and offer me a hundred bucks for my help?! It's hush money, you're a plagiarist, you're a liar. And a fraud and a creep and as of five minutes ago my ex-boyfriend. You think this is funny? Laugh about this: not only do I not want your bribe, or believe your slimy explanation and hey, keep your hands off me! Do not dare to touch me! I'm taking you down, pal. I'm walking my paper over to Student Affairs . . . back off! I trusted you in like nine different ways . . . now it's war.

Performance Notes:

Starts off very, very angry (obviously) but calms down after "shut up, Jason." This is a "worm turns" moment. He has been previously, the dominant partner in the relationship and she is not ordinarily "bossy" or even "loud." Think early Goldie Hawn. She is traditional femininity gone ballistic. She practically screams "whole paragraphs word for word, Jason." But then sits and daintily arranges her spring dress. She retains this composure until " . . . keep your hands off me! Do not dare to touch me!" She now moves toward an imaginary door, turning back to say, "I'm taking you down, pal." The final line is saccharin sweet and she is charmingly smiling. She might even curtsy to him at the end. A great piece for the quiet actress who ordinarily plays "small" to bust out with.

CHANCE

Woman:

See I think I gotta go, Chance. I gotta get out of here because I don't think I'm ready for this. No way am I ready. What do I know about bein' married for instance? I can't cook nuthin' . . . well hardly. Nuthin' where it don't tell ya on the box and even then . . . and the baby? Who knew they don't sleep and they ain't happy? The baby keeps cryin' I wanna slap it, slap it 'til it shuts up and that ain't right. I mean you get a job, you can't do the job, you get fired. That's a rule of life, right? So I gotta fire myself because I suck bad. You know how you get a feelin' a thing won't come to no good end? I got that feelin' Chance, and not that it's your fault, and I'm sayin' you're pretty good to me, you know, most days. I see you love the baby, sing to him, stuff like that and that's what he needs, not that I should slap him like I did today. I slapped him pretty good. So, I'm goin' to my uncle's up in Indianapolis. I stayed around 'til you came home 'cause I should tell you in person, and now I did. I got diapers. I put a casserole kinda thing in the oven. I sold my car and left you the money except what I need for the bus. You're a good guy. You should never a got mixed up with me. Have a good life.

Performance Notes:

This is a specialty piece. If it's right for you it's really right but it's not for everybody. It's probably best with a deep south or "Southie" accent from Boston. The strange reality of this piece is a certain lack of emotion. She knows abstractly she shouldn't slap babies but it doesn't stop her. She's chewing gum and maybe (mime) doing her nails and she talks about her penchant for violence the way you and I might talk about having a cold. She actually smiles when she says, "I slapped him pretty good." She's not really upset with herself even though she realizes her bad behavior. She's pleasant to Chance in the way you might be pleasant to a clerk while buying clothes. She likes Chance, she is simply not tied to him in any romantic way. She knows he likes casseroles so she made him one. Whatever physicality you find should be commonplace. What makes this piece work is the making of an extraordinary and even dangerous personality as ordinary as possible.

SIX

Man:

See, this here is an Indian head nickel from the old days. My daddy he had a bunch of em' and I stole me one. My daddy was a man did everything right. He was a Lutheran and they don't mess around like Catholics do. He was old school right down to the ground. This guy tried to mess around with Mom and Daddy went to Big Time Pawn, bought him a gun, got in a cab over to Pep Boys where the guy worked, walked in, shot him in the balls. Then he asked could he use their phone so he could call the police on himself. He didn't fool around, see. He had him an inner clock about right and wrong, he didn't have to check in *The Bible*. So now, my sister tells me you owe her two hundred dollars, so I told her I'd stop by and get it. Now I'm only going to ask you for it once, which is how they did it in the old school, and I'll be back when I get off work. I keep this nickel with me so I don't forget the right way to do things. So listen up: I want it in fresh twenty dollar bills in a nice white envelope on which you write "Sincere Apologies." That's what my sister deserves, so that's how we'll do it. See you around six. No later.

Performance Notes:

He starts, naturally holding the nickel up above shoulder level where it can be clearly seen. The speaker pockets the nickel after the line, "He was old school right down to the ground. " He/she sits on the next line and then rises on, "So now my sister tells me you owe her two hundred dollars . . ." the next line "now I'm only going to ask you for it once . . ." is the most important in the piece and should be delivered coldly and slowly. Pat your pocket on "I keep this nickel with me . . ." The other dangerous moment is on, "That's what my sister deserves, so that's how we'll do it." The character should wear a baseball cap and touches the bill of the cap with old fashioned courtesy on the last line. This character has no doubt he will get what he wants so he doesn't have to overplay it. There is something leisurely in the characters manner. He has the immense assurance of meaning exactly what he says.

BORING

Woman:

I'm sorry to disappoint you Jack but I cannot completely abandon my rational mind. You're cute, nobody can say you aren't cute, but you are spending way too much time in the bathroom because aliens can't walk on tile. I'm not going into your belief in magnetism, astrology, numerology, phrenology, and the efficacy of frying pine needles as a cure for night blindness. I am your fiancé, Jack. But I don't want to be married by a Universalist minister in the WalMart parking lot. Then, as to the honeymoon, I'm just not up for survivalist war games in Costa Rica. I know I'm a little boring but the truth is I'm a little boring and you are . . . well, you are a nuthatch jack which has been . . . interesting for a year but I have prospects for life. I enjoyed the mushroom hunting and living in the tree, and let's not forget you taking out my appendix with your penknife. So I am returning the pop top that has served as an engagement ring and I am going online and meet a certified public accountant who will carry me over the threshold of a tract home in Toledo.

Performance Notes:

She has to talk very carefully and firmly to Jack because he has a short attention span. Sometimes she has to wave her hands at him so he will look at her. She has tried. She does sort of love him, but he has worn her down with his eccentricities. She's not making jokes because, in fact, he has no sense of humor. She is carefully warm and friendly in her approach, practical but not at all hostile and certainly not angry. Some of her points she ticks off on her fingers like a grocery list. The only moment that is infected with powerful negativity is " . . . interesting for a year but a horrifying prospect for a life." She is in fact . . . well . . horrified. Sometimes she is amazed at her experiences with him as in " . . . taking out my appendix with your penknife." She gets very close to the imaginary Jack and whispers the final works, " . . . I am going online and meeting a certified public accountant who will carry me over the threshold of a tract home in Toledo."

CATWOMAN

Man:

Okay, hey, you have better taste than I do, but deal. I wear orange, arrest me. My favorite movie is *Catwomen on the Moon* and I think the Olive Garden is high end and I want you to get off my back. Love can survive bad taste. . . look at your parents. Seriously, the guy wears a snuggie when he gardens and he watches "300 Days to a Bermuda Bootie" on cable.

And I like him. I trust him. And you can trust me, you know you can. I will be here when I'm needed, wearing orange or whatever, because what is taste compared to commitment? What is a terrible color sense and a Green Lantern comic book collection compared to the very real deal that I would do ANYTHING for you. I will live where you want, I love your faults, I think your lame jokes are hysterical and I will, without question, devote my tasteless self to your every need forever! Hell, you can dress me any way you want, pick the movies and the restaurants, tell me how to vote and choose the sexual positions. I love you. I love you. I love you. Let's not worry about orange.

Performance Notes:

This man has just proposed marriage to a woman who seemed reluctant to say yes. When pressed she mentioned that people who meet him are sometimes put off by his taste. This audition piece is his reply to her. The central line that has to pop out and be remembered by the audience is, " . . . what is taste compared to commitment?" He is convinced she needs him and the action is little in this piece because she is pacing while she tries to think. He drops to one knee on "I love you. I love you. I love you." He puts both hands over his heart as he says, "Let's not worry about orange." There is nothing tasteless about his manor which is sweet and gentlemanly. When he talks about her parents he tries not to offend her. He is, however, wearing some wildly colored Bermudas.

THE MALL

Man:

Ummm, hi. I'm . . . all right, what I think I'm doing, you know, just uh . . . well approaching a perfect stranger in a mall . . . barging in on your . . . is that a cinnamon pretzel? I love cinnamon pretzels . . . all right, okay, what I'm doing here is uh . . . is uh . . . okay, what I'm doing is flat out, unabashedly, without apology, very directly. . . hitting on you, coming on to you, with uh . . . with uh . . . what you're mother would call questionable motives. Because this is . . . okay, hard to say this . . . this is . . . this kind of weird approach is entirely . . and I apologize for this . . . sexually driven . . . which is probably not cool to admit but come on, look at you for God's sake . . . you are a mall goddess, the lips, the legs, the rack, the waist length blonde hair . . . I mean a guy wouldn't come over here to discuss literature! So ummm, I wondered if I could kiss you . . . not here . . . not here in the mall but at some prearranged place of your choice at a time convenient to you. So that's why I came over here. Ow! Okay, let's just say this didn't work out. On the other hand you aren't leaving.

Performance Notes:

Well, the first thing that needs talking about is all those dot, dot, dots (. . .). The character needs to think before they speak again and so do you. The pause could be one beat or three beats but it needs to be there. In this case they also indicate the speaker is nervous, unsure of himself, perhaps embarrassed which is a key to unlocking the monologue. He's not used to doing this and he's a little clumsy. Several times he considers just breaking off and leaving the battlefield but then like a wounded soldier, he just staggers on. Finally he just blurts out, "so, ummm, I wondered if I could kiss you . . ." and immediately slaps his forehead for having said it. One of the reasons he doesn't leave is that after a while she finds his clumsiness amusing and at the end, before his last line, gives him the kind of smile that is at least good for a cup of coffee. That last line of his is part amazement that it might be working out

Sweet Revenge

Woman:

This is insulting. There is nothing about this that works

for me. You don't have the time for me? You had the time for me in bed. You had time to do your little dance of seduction. You had time to explain in detail how you were separated from the wife you're not separated from. And now you have the time to explain to me for two hours that you don't have time? Hey, I'm not your mother. I don't do your schedule but I will tell you what I have time for. I have time to cause you a world of hurt. I have time to go over to your house and tell your pudgy little wife what's been going on since January. You think since you're thirty and I'm nineteen I'm a helpless baby? My apartment's wired Alan, and I have the whole sound score of your very demonstrative performances with me, which I'm also sending to your parents, your boss and a friend of mine who does stand-up comedy. See Alan, this is what they used to call revenge and is it going to feel good? Oh, yes it is! I am going to dance and holler. Want to see me dance! Yes! Yes! Yes! Yes! Yes! Yes!! I'd show you the whole thing but I just don't have time for you. Eat dirt and die, sucker.

Performance Notes:

This is pretty rough. Not for everybody and certainly not for all nineteen year olds . . . Still it might have the edgy quality you've been looking for. Sometimes that quality jolts those auditioning you back to consciousness. The speaker has begun to doubt that there is anything in this for the guy except the sex. She has waited for him outside his office and he has tried to blow her off with a lame excuse. That's where the piece starts. She starts out confused and then her anger begins to heat up and it builds to a peak on the line "I have time to cause you a world of hurt." Seeing some people passing by she pulls it down to a low tone which she keeps until, "See Alan, this is what they used to call revenge . . . " which gets louder, peaking with "Yes! Yes! Yes! Yes! Yes!!" She then smiles a nasty, cold smile while being politely vicious and stands on her tip-toes to whisper the last line in his ear.

WHITE CHRISTMAS

Man or Woman:

Holy Moly . . . oh my goodness . . . ummm, I uh . . . you probably wonder why I'm uhh . . . uhh . . . standing on your porch in a blizzard at uh . . . three in the morning. Actually, I wonder why I'm standing on your porch at three in the morning. And your parents really wonder, because I saw the lights go on upstairs . . . and the neighbors wonder . . . The guy in his pajamas with the uh . . . the uh . . . the shotgun across the street, he's scary and uh . . . okay, this is what demented love looks like. Unrequited demented love which I am standing on your porch with really wet feet to declare. All right, now we have a silence, right? You're silent, I'm silent because we have no idea ummm, what to say. Do we? We don't. Right. So, I am going home now. See me going? And uh . . . sorry I woke you up, shotgun guy! You look great . . . and I hate that. Bye now. Just uh, tell your parents I'm demented. Because I am . . . obviously. What on earth have I done? Oh well. Bye now.

Performance Notes:

Okay, it's cold. And not just for the first two lines and then we forget about it. It's cold all the way to "Bye now." If I were you I'd make a list of cold activities. Your arms hugging your chest, rubbing your nose for warmth, foot stamping, etc. You should have at least seven or eight. It gives the piece a wonderful physicality. Also it's three in the morning. Picture your love object at the door wrapped in a blankey. You start regretting knocking on the door the minute you see her/him. The first words, "Holy Moly" are active regret. You really have gone a little crazy, but you can't stop. The speaker might hit himself/herself three or four times during the piece. He punishes himself even while he can't stop. In a sense he 'sobers up, or gets calm' around, "So I am going home now." The rest of the piece is less manic. "And I hate that," is his/her last outburst. "What on earth have I done" is said slowly, amazed. And it's cold. Don't forget it's cold.

Jon Jory

Man or Woman:

Excuse me . Hey. Excuse me! Hey!! Sorry but I did put up my hand. See, hand up? Now wait, you called on me. When I said "Hey!!" Hold it! Look, I have been trying not to say this all year . . . if you can't say anything nice don't say anything at all, right? But listen, this is serious, you are a really, really terrible teacher. Terrible. Terrible! So sorry. So sorry but I am the consumer, right? I buy you and you suck. Sorry. You are disorganized, you are repetitive, you have twice fallen asleep while you were talking! For real, dude . . . asleep! And, so sorry, your dandruff . . . your dandruff . . . when you get excited you look like a snow globe. Wait. Wait. I still have the floor. You need to shine your shoes, man . . . clean your breakfast off your mustache, stop picking your nose. We're discussing Egypt, man, the greatest culture in human history and you are melting my brain! I'm sorry. Let Marsha over there teach the class she knows this stuff and we can pretend we're getting an education! Sorry. Sorry. Are you crying? Tell me you're not crying!? I'm an animal. I'm a monster. Class over, let's go get a beer.

Performance Notes:

The speaker isn't an "animal" he's a freshman in college running up $60,000 in student loans before he graduates and he really wants an education! The outburst is unplanned, it's spontaneous and needs to feel that way. He/she keeps apologizing because he really didn't plan to do this. The pace in the early going is quick. His brain is way ahead of his words. Work fast but let your head keep changing directions like a motorcycle racer. For some illogical reason the dandruff really gets him! He hates dandruff! It repels him! Starting with "you need to shine your shoes, man . . . " he gets relative control of himself and speaks slowly and distinctly. He lets go vocally on" . . . and we can pretend we're getting an education!" Then he stops dead. Solid pause before "Sorry."

"I'm an animal. I'm a monster" is a whisper. Pause. Last line is directed at the whole class.

Who?

Man or Woman:

So, you asked me, so I'll tell you but to be honest you're not going to like it very much and I have no idea, none if you really want to know anything about yourself because, to be perfectly honest you seem almost totally absent from your own life. You're like a performance of a Jake of your imagination, all sweet and funny and concerned and sincere and positive and certain of your own sexuality and I don't believe it, and I've tried. You don't cast a shadow, Jake. There's no dark about you anywhere. You're like Santa all year long and it makes me avert my eyes because it's so embarrassing and made up and the idea that anybody is fooled Jake, is just brutally sad because you're in there somewhere but you just won't let yourself out, and I don't care if you're gay or a serial murderer or the poster child for the witness protection program, I just need to know who is in there? And don't make a joke. I'll kill you if you make a joke. Just show up.

Performance Notes:

To be frank this is part of a conversation that probably takes place after more than a couple of beers. These two have known each other for at least a couple of years. The speaker has become convinced that Jake has some kind of secret life. She recently heard from someone she knows that he was in New York, and as far as she knows he's never been out of Arizona. She's been waiting to bring this up. She never meets his friends, he never talks about his family or his past. Who is he? To start with he asks if she loves him and the piece is off and running. Most of this piece is done sitting. She gets up and moves behind her chair on," . . . because you're in there somewhere . . . ." What really defines the piece are the long sentences, particularly the one starting, "You're like Santa all year long . . . " so choose where you will take your breaths. She's fed up but it isn't anger as much as regret. She cares for him but there are things she needs to know. It's now or never. Spread the words" . . . who-is-in-there?" A burst of anger (the only one) on "And don't make a joke. I'll kill you if you make a joke." And then warm, even hopeful on, "Just show up."

9:20

Man or Woman:

Nine twenty p.m., Wednesday, September fifteenth, here it is again. The exact minute our father shot our mother and then himself and left us a note saying he was "sorry." So I thought I would call you and see how you are doing because I'm not doing too well. Not too well at all, but you're not there . . . as you often aren't, so here I am talking to technology instead of you which, actually, is probably better because otherwise I'd be crying and I'm really sick of crying and I think it's making a grand canyon on my face. So, let's see, the wisteria died. Sorry, black thumb. I have a new, used car . . . I forget what make. I'm a vegetarian now and I have a sort of significant other who I don't consider too significant. Listen, I wonder now that time has passed and the river of life rolls on if you have any idea why he did it? Hope so. Call back. I'll be up 'til I finish the bottle of vodka. Anything would help I think. Love you. Bye.

Performance Notes:

Family is "blood" and we turn to blood for answers or just to ask questions, right? The speaker is calling on the anniversary of his/her father's death. Obviously he/she feels terrible. The secret of making a depressed state stage worthy is to fight it, not to give in to it. When he speaks of not "doing well" he means today not yesterday. So, try to keep an open, rational tone and then drop it down into something more emotional for a line or two, (only once or twice) not more. There's even a little sense of humor from "So here I am talking to technology not you . . . " through "grand canyon on my face." Make sure also that it isn't all in a measured, gloomy rhythm, find a quick part, vary the pace. Take a pause before, "Anytime would help I think. (that's a dark moment)." Most importantly vary the tone.

BRIAN

Woman:

Why don't I get angry? Well, it's nice you finally asked, Brian. It's nice being noticed, particularly because we're engaged. Unless we're not engaged. Are we still engaged? Because you so seldom talk to me I'M JUST NOT SURE! See, that qualifies as anger but I don't often indulge myself because you get mad and then I get mad and then we yell and break things and then, Brian, a deafening silence descends like a morning mist over San Francisco. And while we don't often talk, when we do talk, you make strange faces as if a gopher was trying to eat it's way out through your face. Until finally, several days later, you can't find your car keys and then you say you love me, and have I seen your car keys and then I get mad and you get mad and we throw things and yell. So actually, I'm not angry, but I'm not marrying you. Whoa! Is that you looking relieved? Okay Brian, now I'm angry! How dare you look relieved when I say I'm not marrying you?! And don't tell me I'm angry, I know I'm angry!

Performance Notes:

Of course she is angry though she says she isn't. The pace is generally brisk because she doesn't want to be interrupted or hear what he has to say. In the middle you'll note there is a very long sentence which you have to do in as close to one breath as possible. Remember that toward the end she says,

"Okay Brian, now I'm angry!" and she's the angriest we see, so you have to keep most of the early stuff under control. Remember also that the piece starts in the middle of a conversation not the start and her emotions are already building though she still has some control over them. Make sure you play this scene with the imaginary Brian. See when he moves. Respond when he . . . well . . . gives you the imaginary finger. Tone your performance to what this Brian does while you are talking. Those judging you will admire that.

SHIRTS

Man:

Yeah, I watch stuff. Who comes, who goes, and I remember; I know some people want to know stuff and I'm, most times, available with the stuff they want to know. Kind of a specialty I got which is available for payment, if you see what I mean? Me and this guy Duke, we go down, watch the trawlers come in, watch the pleasure boats, watch guys fishing but that ain't work that's entertainment to take care of the stress I got tryin' to remember the stuff I see. An' I seen you. Seen you down here before an' you don't look quite right, okay? I got this eye, see, and you got the wrong shirt, you got the wrong shoes which altogether is a cop look. Am I right? You know I'm right. So I will communicate this what I see to my payin' customers, an' a bunch a bad stuff will come down you don't want to participate in, believe me. Take my word for it. So if I was you, I would give me five, ten bucks for seein' you before the bad guys an' tippin' you off, right? An' don't wear no fake-ass bowling shirt you come down here again. Look around you, sucker, you think my people bowl?

Performance Notes:

The guy speaking is a police informant but in this case he's dealing with another man whose behavior is flat out suspicious. The speaker is always looking to make a buck.

He sees an opportunity and he's all over it. This probably takes place in a neighborhood bar. The speaker keeps his voice down and checks, more than once, to insure no one is listening. The speaker has a quick, nervous manner speaking right in the other man's face. At the end he notices people are staring and he uses the last two sentences to satisfy their interest. It's the only time he raises his voice. The nervous energy that is his trademark means that even when he's standing still he shuffles his feet, bobs forward and back at the waist as if he was listening to music. He's pretty obviously on something. He's cocky and worried almost in the same moment. Enjoy him.